CELEBRATING

70

Mark McGwire's historic season

Editorial Direction

RON SMITH

Design

BILL WILSON

Photographic Coordination

ALBERT DICKSON

Prepress Project Coordinator

DAVID BRICKEY

Co-written by

BERNIE MIKLASZ
RON SMITH
MIKE EISENBATH
DAVE KINDRED

CONTRIBUTORS

Editorial Directors

Steve Meyerhoff, *The Sporting News;* Bob Rose, *St. Louis Post-Dispatch;*
Mike Smith, *St. Louis Post-Dispatch.*

Chief Copy Editor

Tom Klein, *St. Louis Post-Dispatch*

Copy Editors/Researchers

Todd Fitzpatrick, *The Sporting News;* Leslie Gibson McCarthy, *The Sporting News;*
Brendan Roberts, *The Sporting News;* Steve Siegel, *The Sporting News;*
Dave Sloan, *The Sporting News;* George Winkler, *The Sporting News.*

Graphics and Design

Ken Amos, *The Sporting News;* Amy Beadle, *The Sporting News;*
Michael Behrens, *The Sporting News.*

Prepress Director

Michael Bruner, *The Sporting News.*

Prepress Specialists

Steve Romer, *The Sporting News;* Ian Wilkinson, *The Sporting News.*

Contents

Foreword

by Jack Buck

It didn't take long

to plot the course for a memorable 1998 season. After four games, Mark McGwire had four home runs. At the end of May he had 27. By June 12, 65 games into the schedule for his St. Louis Cardinals, McGwire was halfway to the magic 62 figure that would make him the greatest single-season home run hitter of all time.

Strewn along the path of Big Mac's historic march were dramatic moments, 500-foot skidmarks, shellshocked pitchers and more standing ovations than a humble American folk hero could possibly endure. Waiting for him at the end was the emotional embrace of adoring fans and the unexpected challenge of Chicago Cubs right fielder Sammy Sosa, the shadow that wouldn't go away.

It was the perfect season for the near-perfect sports hero. And McGwire didn't shrink from his appointed rounds. He handled the media storm with calm and class, he charmed a nation with his values and humility and he helped baseball find forgiveness and rejuvenation with every powerful sweep of his bat.

Never in my 48 years in baseball had I seen anything like it. It was the most amazing thing, unparalleled— and not just in St. Louis. It was everywhere we went. It enveloped everybody in baseball, including all the Cardinals greats who rooted him on. McGwire brought everybody together, from Ozzie Smith to Bob Gibson, Lou Brock and Stan Musial. It was really fun to watch.

The following pages provide a homer-by-homer record of Mac's incredible journey. It's a celebration of the man as much as his feat. Every McGwire home run is captured photographically, but the ups and downs,

the highs and lows, the drama and routine of an exhausting season are captured in the words and pictures of The Sporting News and St. Louis Post-Dispatch reporters who were there.

The final chapter of this fascinating story deals with the race—the riveting Sosa-McGwire stretch run for baseball's single-season home run record after

THE DAY AFTER: *The McGwire aura took on a new dimension at Cincinnati's Cinergy Field the day after historic home run No. 62 .*

McGwire had won the sprint to 62. But when all was said and done, the final chapter was really the beginning of a more enduring relationship between baseball and its prodigal fans.

That's a message McGwire delivered over and over with every ovation and roar he generated during a historic season. The Summer of '98.

Jack Buck

The Summer of '98

*Mark McGwire's power and magnetism
rejuvenated an ailing game*

Mark McGwire was riding in the back of a taxi, en route to Pittsburgh's Three Rivers Stadium, when he saw the police barricades. Hundreds of fans waited behind the sealed-off area near the players' entrance. They had stood for hours, patiently waiting to get a glimpse of their generation's Babe Ruth.

With four hours remaining before the scheduled first pitch, McGwire's green eyes twinkled in disbelief. He stepped out of the cab—the reason why so many had come so early, the reason why the stadium would be sold out on consecutive nights for the first time in 28 years, the reason why fans were falling in love with baseball again.

Cameras clicked. Mothers and fathers lifted their children to see him. Fans shouted McGwire's name, pleading for his autograph. Kids squealed.

"We love you Mark!"

"Hit one tonight!"

"Get the record, Mac!"

McGwire smiled and waved. Two security men rushed to his side and led him to the safety of the Cardinals' clubhouse. McGwire exhaled. This display of unconditional love had taken his breath away.

"Never in my wildest dreams," McGwire said, "did I ever think something like this would ever happen to me."

It was like this at every stop as McGwire barnstormed through the summer. St. Louis was his home base, his seat of power. But as he began sending home runs to the constellations, it became obvious: McGwire was much too large to be confined to one city, and no single ballpark could contain him. St. Louis understood, and America's best baseball town happily shared McGwire with the rest of the nation.

In the summer of 1998, baseball became a hit again—a home run that landed in the traditional soft spot of our national heritage. And more than any other player, McGwire was responsible for picking up the ailing game, slinging it across his wide shoulders and carrying it into living rooms across the country.

Mac got help in the season's first half from Seattle center fielder Ken Griffey Jr., who kept pace in the home-run fusillade. And when Griffey dropped off, a new power emerged: Chicago Cubs outfielder Sammy Sosa, who became McGwire's home-running mate in a joyful competition that charmed and captivated fans around the world. But if Sosa was baseball's middleweight champion, McGwire ruled the heavyweight division. He hit more homers, longer homers, and grabbed the larger share of headlines and attention.

When Big Mac came to town, it was a civic event. McGwire's batting practice was the best warmup act in sports. All across America, he hit cannon balls and took curtain calls. He pounded baseballs. He pounded baseball's bad image. The game was a brighter place, illuminated by a thousand camera flashes—those beautiful points of light—when he swung the bat.

"You're never going to see anything like him," said Cardinals broadcaster Mike Shannon, who has been with the team as a player and a radio voice since 1962. "In Mark McGwire, what you're talking about is John Wayne, Paul Bunyan and Superman rolled into one."

McGwire brought the fans back. And he brought families together, including his own. When McGwire hit his record-tying 61st homer, his father was in the seats at Busch Stadium, celebrating his 61st birthday. McGwire looked behind home plate and shouted, "Happy Birthday, Dad!" And McGwire's 10-year-old son, Matthew, observed the drama from his on-field perch as a Cardinals batboy. Three generations unified by one homer.

McGwire's feats became a shared interest between parents and children. Breakfast-table discussions

centered around box scores and McGwire's home-run tote board. At night, the families who couldn't watch or listen together provided home-run bulletins for each other with urgent phone calls.

The kids were wild about Big Mac. His stadium-rattling homers looked like something straight out of their video games and he bore a striking resemblance to the action figures that dominated afternoon television. It was cool the way he let his son hang with him at the ballpark, and how he fulfilled Matthew's spring-training prediction of 65 homers. He fought for other kids, too, donating $1 million annually to the foundation he established to combat child abuse.

Parents treasured him because he stressed the value of hard work, dedication and team-first play. And he shared himself, with remarkable grace. We especially were moved by the way McGwire reached out to the sons and daughters of the late Roger Maris, retroactively giving them the affection that had eluded their tormented father in 1961, when he defied New York's

wishes and broke Ruth's single-season home run record.

One August day at St. Louis' Busch Stadium, as McGwire left the field after batting practice, he looked into the stands. A 5-year-old boy was holding up a sign: "Hey Mark, It's My Birthday." McGwire walked over and handed the wide-eyed boy his first baseman's glove. There were similar scenes in other stadiums.

McGwire was the superhero that baseball needed after the destructive strike of 1994. But he was real. And he went from town to town spreading home runs, souvenirs and goodwill. Catcher Tom Lampkin, his teammate and friend, called McGwire's tour a "traveling salvation show."

And he was fun. The epic nature of his rocket-blast home runs satisfied our national craving for big, bigger, biggest. If you want to diagram the flight pattern of a typical McGwire homer, use St. Louis' Gateway Arch as your model.

McGwire's home runs dented signs and scoreboards at Busch Stadium. He caused $5,000 worth of damage to

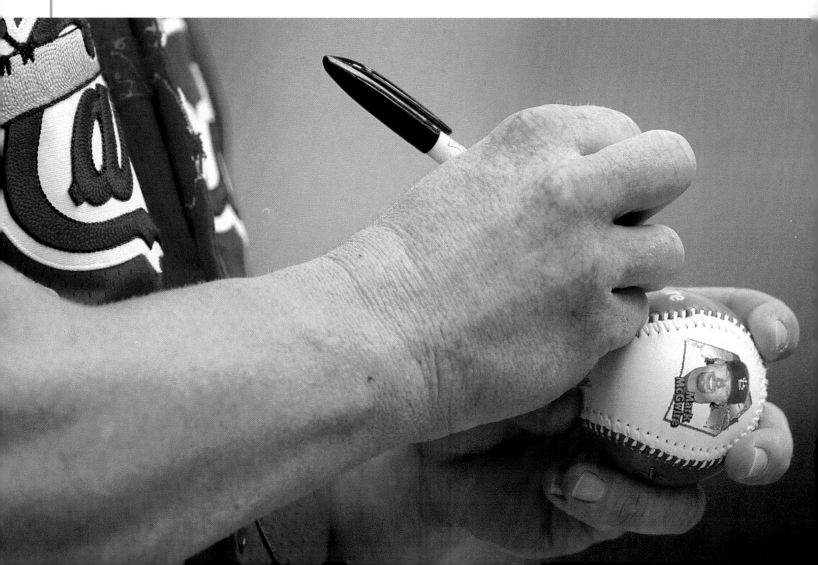

CROWD CONTROL: *With McGwire looking for home run No. 60, pregame activity outside Busch Stadium became a shoulder-bumping hazard.*

EVERYWHERE A SIGN: *Every direction McGwire turned, he encountered hordes of photographers, reporters and autograph-seeking fans. He tried hard to accommodate everybody and even tossed a few bones to the crowd.*

the scoreboard in Arizona. He struck a car in the players' parking lot at Coors Field in Colorado. He plunked a batting-practice ball off a bus on Waveland Avenue, beyond the left field bleachers at Chicago's Wrigley Field. He hit a stadium usher with an upper-deck batting-practice shot in Miami. He was dangerous.

"People say Babe Ruth hit them this way," Mets catcher Mike Piazza said. "But I really can't believe that Babe Ruth could hit them higher or longer than McGwire."

Rare is the athlete who consistently satisfies and delights the paying customer. But McGwire sent legions of babbling, bubbly people home from the ballpark to tell next-day tales of 500-foot homers around the coffee pot, or on the front steps of their church.

McGwire touched them all, young and old. Grandmothers baked him

cookies. Grandfathers reminisced about baseball's good old days. Women sent him flowers. Kids pretended to be McGwire in their backyard games, launching the ball, just like Big Mac, over the rooftops.

McGwire emerged as a pop-culture curiosity. He attracted visits from celebrities, including Bruce Springsteen, Jerry Seinfeld, Tommy Hilfiger, Brett Favre, Dan Marino and other professional athletes. Sarah Ferguson, the Duchess of York, sat behind the Cardinals' dugout at Wrigley Field one day, waving an autographed McG-

wire bat.

"He's my favorite redhead," Fergie declared.

McGwire was baseball's equivalent of Michael Jordan. Everyone wanted to touch him, see him. And he responded with a natural showman's flair for the dramatic, an impeccable sense of timing.

On opening day, his grand slam knocked out the Dodgers. On April 14, Matthew made his season debut as a batboy and big daddy homered three times to destroy Arizona. On July 11, a slumping McGwire asked Matthew to kiss his bat for good luck, then walloped a 485-foot homer that zapped Houston and closer Billy Wagner. On August 19 in Chicago, Sosa hit his 48th home run to take

a 1-stroke lead over McGwire, who allowed him to stay on top for exactly 58 minutes. Then Mac cranked two homers in the same game to reclaim the lead.

They left the park at a consistently furious pace. By the end of April, he had 11. By the end of May, he was resting on 27. June ended at 37, July closed at 45 and August at 55—one away from Hack Wilson's National League record and the homestretch of his remarkable quest—toward an eventual, unfathomable 70.

As he made his final approach to the record, McGwire's clutch touch was tested again. The Cardinals opened a five-game homestand September 4 with McGwire sitting on 59 home runs. He desperately wanted to bang three more and set the record in front of his adoring St. Louis fans.

Home run No. 60, which put him in company with the immortal Ruth, came in

Game 2 of the stand against the Cincinnati Reds. Homer 61, the Maris equalizer, came two days later, in a Labor Day showdown with the Cubs. He had one game left, one more chance to reward the city that had embraced him so lovingly and enthusiastically.

The date: September 8, 1998.

The time: 8:18 p.m.

With two out in the fourth inning, McGwire attacked the first pitch from Cubs starter Steve Trachsel. His 62nd home run was a streak of lightning. We barely had time to register the history that flashed before our eyes. The shot surged down the left field line, only 341 feet away, and barely cleared the wall in the corner as his shortest homer of the year.

Hey, why delay the celebration with a long-descending 500-footer? McGwire delivered, and Busch Stadium staged a nationally televised house party.

KEEP YOUR EYE ON THE BALL: *Under the watchful eye of Chicago rival Sammy Sosa (left), other fascinated players and thousands of McGwire-hungry fans, Big Mac put on a daily batting-practice show that played to rave reviews all over the country.*

"So much has been put on this guy," Cardinals manager Tony La Russa said. "Everywhere he goes, he's the center of attention. He's been given the responsibility for carrying the game on his shoulders. And I watch him thinking, 'There's no way we can expect one man to deliver like this. It's too much to ask. It isn't fair.' He has an anvil on his back. And then he swings the bat, and the ball goes over the fence. It's overwhelming."

But make no mistake, the home-run mission was never as easy as McGwire made it seem. Through the final month and a half, he had to deal with a serious challenge from the irrepressible Sosa, who stalked him down to the final weekend and made Mac's fans sweat through every swing.

Mac and Sammy, seemingly linked at the biceps, assaulted history together. And their duel brought out the best in each man. If Sosa homered, McGwire would respond. When McGwire pulled into a seemingly comfortable lead, Sosa would catch up with a stunning barrage. They exchanged these long-distance telegrams and

spectators packed ballparks at every stop, standing and straining to see every precious at-bat.

It was gripping theater, but not the only entertainment they provided. Mac and Sammy raised the level of sportsmanship on our playing fields. There was no trash talk or finger pointing and they openly rooted for each other. The shared experience drew them closer and they became fast friends, not hated foes. They were baseball's equivalent of Magic Johnson vs. Larry Bird.

Sosa was in right field when McGwire slipped No. 62 over the Busch Stadium wall in left. He ran in to embrace McGwire, who wrapped him in a bear hug. And then they exchanged their favorite post-homer rituals: McGwire threw playful punches to the stomach and Sosa blew kisses.

When McGwire made the comment, "Wouldn't it be great if we finished in a tie," no one smirked. We believed him, because Sosa and McGwire had a genuine camaraderie. And while chasing one of the most cherished records in all of sports, they cleaned up some pol-

lution on the professional landscape.

What an unlikely duo:
McGwire, the son of a California
dentist who grew up near
Disneyland; Sosa, the poor kid
from the Dominican Republic who
sold oranges and shined shoes to
support his family after the death
of his father.

Baseball brought McGwire and
Sosa together.
And they brought
baseball back to
its feel-good past.

We tingled
through the final
weeks, after Sosa
had paused at 58
homers, allowing
McGwire to reach
62 first. But Mac wasn't home
free, not by a long shot.

Emotionally deflated after
passing Maris, McGwire went a
week without homering, and the
opportunistic Sosa caught him at
62 with a dramatic four-homer
weekend bombardment against
Milwaukee at Wrigley Field.
That's when the real race began.
Sosa caught McGwire again at 63
and again at 65, thanks to another
two-homer game against the Brewers on the
final Wednesday of the season. And then, on
the last Friday of the season, Sammy took another 1-stroke lead—for 45 minutes.

Sosa refused to go away and pushed
McGwire to the end—a fitting conclusion to a
remarkable season. In sports, the only way to
certify greatness is to defeat greatness, the
way Muhammad Ali fed off Joe Frazier,
Affirmed responded to Alydar and the Lakers
finally overcame the Celtics.

McGwire needed Sosa. But
Sammy wasn't the only barrier.

During one grumpy stretch after
the All-Star break, a mentally and
physically fatigued McGwire re-
sisted his own celebrity. He tried
to disassemble his own band-
wagon. He yearned for solitude,
away from the autograph requests
and the demands for interviews.
Around midseason, flecks of gray
appeared on his red goatee.

And this was appropriate; the
personal angst gave him an extension to Maris. The proper
historical connections were
now established: McGwire,
like Ruth, was an extra-large
slugger who hit special-effects
homers. McGwire, like Maris,
squirmed in the public petri
dish. To become baseball's new
home run king, McGwire
would need
Babe's physical
strength and
Roger's mental
fortitude.

McGwire's link
to Ruth and Maris
seemingly gave
him peace. As he
closed in on
Ruth's 60 and Maris' 61, he felt
them in his heart. He talked of
wanting to meet them in
heaven. And he offered this elo-
quent monologue—spoken
September 5 after his 60th
home run—as what he would
say to Ruth and Maris, if given
a chance:

"I would ask them if they
ever felt the way I'm feeling
right now.

"I would ask them if their heart beat a mile
a minute, the way my heart is racing now.

"I'd ask them if the emotions ran through
them, the way my emotions are right now. I
have this incredible feeling inside. Did they
feel this way, too?

"I would ask them how their life was away
from the field, and if they could relax.

"I'd ask them about the media back then,
and how it compared to what I'm going
through now.

"I'd ask them how the
pitchers were, what they faced,
what was tough about hitting
in their time.

"I'd ask them about the guys
they played with, their teammates, and if they were as
great as mine are now.

"I would ask them if they re-
alized at the time that all of
America was watching, the
way I feel all the eyes are

TONY AWARD: *Despite McGwire's long professional relationship with Tony La Russa (below right), everything he accomplished during the Summer of '98 amazed and impressed the Cardinals manager.*

watching me now.

"There's so much I'd want to talk to them about. And one day I will."

As soon as he overcame his emotional blockage, McGwire was home free. When he released his heart to America, it liberated him to make history.

As sports fans, we want our stars to have a human touch. When McGwire digs into the batter's box, he is as imposing as the Colossus of Rhodes. But there's vulnerable tissue under all those muscles.

McGwire has a bulging disk in his back. He has 20/500 eyesight. He has weak arches and wears a special shoe insert to keep his feet aligned. He has had three surgeries on his heels. His sinuses drip. McGwire has endured the agony of divorce. He went through psychological counseling to overcome a confidence crisis.

We could relate when an overly excited McGwire had to backtrack and touch first base to correct a misstep after his 62nd homer. Wouldn't you be dizzy, too? He aches, he stumbles—but he grinds on. Such visible adversity makes him even more endearing to everyday people.

"I've had enough adversity in my personal life, and in my professional life," McGwire said. "It would have been easy for me to turn around and to never be heard of again. But I decided to bust through the walls. My life has not been easy. I'm a perfect example of a person who is normal, who can conquer things if they can dream and believe in themselves."

Through all of the emotion and unrelenting acclaim, McGwire never stopped thinking of others. His press conferences in each city usually included a cheer-up message to those experiencing rough times. His pursuit of the record turned into a national parade, and he ignited the fireworks with his bat. He wanted everyone to join him, even those seemingly forgotten by society.

McGwire Mania was officially embraced as a national phenomenon August 20 at Shea Stadium in New York. McGwire homered in the first game of a doubleheader against the Mets, giving him 50 for the season and a major league record—no player had ever popped 50 homers for three consecutive seasons. As he rounded first base, he pumped his fists, clapped his hands; he paused at

the dugout to salute the cheering New York fans.

Big Mac put the Big Apple in his pocket.

Later that night, a thankful McGwire took a few cartons of baseballs to his hotel room and stayed awake until the wee small hours of the morning, personalizing autographed keepsakes for his teammates. He would do it again after hitting No. 62, scribbling on baseballs through the night to give his friends a piece of memorabilia, straight from his heart. "As great as he is as a player," La Russa said, "he's even a better person."

And he brought out the best in us, too. Late in the season, as he hit the various milestones of his record run, it was startling to see fans return the home run balls to McGwire, resisting the temptation to cash them in for a hefty ransom. He had that effect on people.

In the summer of 1998, Mark McGwire's home runs soared deep into our national consciousness. He hit those homers so high, so far, that they elevated the American spirit.

Bernie Miklasz is a sports columnist for the St. Louis Post-Dispatch.

The batting practice

THE KING OF SWING: *When McGwire takes batting practice, everybody listens—for the crack of the bat that comes with every ball he cranks into the upper deck of Busch Stadium and other big-league parks.*

It's not just for practice anymore.

Not when Mark McGwire steps into the cage.

Cardinals batting practice has become an event—whether McGwire is at Busch Stadium, or any other ballpark in America—something bordering on a rock concert. There's a certain choreography to it, with everything scheduled and no genuine surprises about what is supposed to take place.

But there also is an air of anticipation. Fans expect McGwire to play all the hits, cranked up to full blast, yet the live show always has a fresh feel.

Even if McGwire simply is jamming at rehearsal. The hype lets fans at every ballpark in America know a unique happening will be arriving at the ballpark. Thousands show up much earlier than normal. As soon as the gates open, fans flow down the aisles.

The crowds gather quickly and heavily in two prime locations: at the far corner of the Cardinals' dugout, because fans know McGwire almost always stops there to sign autographs on his way to the bat rack, and anywhere in left field, where chances are good they might come within diving distance of snaring one of the big

phenomenon

redhead's towering drives.

"I've been doing this for 11 years, and no one ever made a big deal out of it before," a baffled McGwire said.

Suddenly, fans are making a big deal out of his every move. The routine finds people booing when he bunts the first pitch, groaning when he "only" smacks a hard line drive into left field or a fly ball that falls short of the fence, and screaming wildly

A CAGED LION: *Cardinal teammates like Ron Gant (left photo, right) found McGwire's batting-practice act fun, but tough to follow. But fans never tired of his prodigious home runs or friendly, accessible manner.*

when he sends a ball soaring into the upper reaches of the park.

Coach Dave McKay, who has thrown thousands of McGwire home runs in BP with Oakland and the Cardinals, has to make sure he fires pitches precisely on the outside part of the plate. McGwire has to lock in and try to please the fans with at least eight homers, which is only a regular day for him.

Players from the opposing team become fans, always making sure they're on the field during the show. Oh, they try to look busy by stretching or playing catch. But they are more like little boys during McGwire's 20 or so batting-practice swings.

And why not? They want to see baseballs soar in the heavens, too.

SHOWTIME: *McGwire's batting-practice routine included stretching, playful moments with teammates and coach Dave Parker (left) and the much-anticipated cage time, sometimes under the supervision of son Matt (above).*

Henry Rodriguez, Chicago Cubs:

"I made sure I wasn't in the clubhouse when he was taking batting practice. I wanted to be in that dugout, out there like everyone else. They want to see him swing. He's the King Kong of baseball. Everybody likes to watch somebody like that. He's a monster."

Ron Gant, St. Louis Cardinals:

"It's different taking batting practice in the same group as him. You go up there trying to hit the ball as far as he can, and you don't even come 150 feet close to it. That can be embarrassing if you think about it, because so many people are watching when you're in his group.

"But it's all in fun. I've always been able to get my work in, and I've been hitting in the same group as him a lot this year. It hasn't changed my batting practice at all.

"But I watch him where I don't always watch other guys I hit with. Even if I hit in the group before he does, I'll stay and watch his group hit. That's something you're not going to see for a long time."

The men who came before

It all starts with Babe Ruth, the ever-immortal Bambino who continues to dominate the baseball record books more than six decades after his final major league season.

When Ruth brought the home run into vogue in the 1920s and punctuated his amazing power feats with a 60-homer assault in 1927, nobody knew what plateaus might be within his reach. The

number 60, it turned out, became magical in baseball lore and the target at which all future generations of power hitters would set their sights.

Several flirted with destiny, but

only one completed his mission. Roger Maris, daring to challenge the immortal Babe while wearing the same Yankees pinstripes and playing in the House That Ruth Built, battled teammate Mickey Mantle through a dramatic 1961 campaign in which the M&M boys powered 115 home runs—a record 61 by Maris and 54 by Mantle, the New York fans' favorite son.

The season was difficult for Maris, who reluctantly sacrificed his privacy to the media blitz that accompanies immortality. New York

BIG HITS: *The Ruth swing (left page) set an enduring standard in 1927, but the Maris home run routine (above, left) played to mixed reviews in the same New York market 34 years later.*

MEMORIES: *Ruth, immortalized (left) by a Hall of Fame plaque that Maris never earned, is greeted at the plate by teammate Lou Gehrig (below right) after a 1927 home run.*

SOUL MATES: *Ruth had Lou Gehrig (above left) and Maris had Mickey Mantle (right) protecting them in the 1927 and 1961 Yankee lineups.*

fans resented Maris challenging their beloved Ruth, commissioner Ford Frick issued his infamous asterisk ruling (to get the record, Maris would have to hit his 61 in 154 games, the schedule Ruth played in 1927) and the media badgered him relentlessly, causing his hair to fall out by season's end. But he persevered and hit his record home run on the final day of the season against Boston.

Maris, who never again would approach such a lofty plateau in a career that fell short of Hall of Fame recognition, had his record, asterisk or not. It would last 37 years, three more than the span Ruth held the mark (1927-61).

The Homers

"KING OF SWING"

1

"How can you not get chills? I was juiced up. I don't know my own strength. I hope I don't hurt anybody."

—McGwire

Two out, bases loaded in the fifth inning of a scoreless battle at Busch Stadium. Los Angeles Dodgers righthander Ramon Martinez, trying to block out memories of the fastball McGwire had transformed into a dramatic 517-foot home run in September 1997, delivers a 1-0 changeup and unwittingly sets the tone for a dramatic and unforgettable St. Louis summer.

Not only did McGwire begin his pursuit of Roger Maris' single-season home run record by launching a majestic 364-foot moonshot into the left field seats, he also served notice that all the preseason hype, all the long-discussed speculation about Ruthian-like feats and special moments, would be addressed in short order. The grand slam, the first ever by a Cardinals player on opening day, was delivered to a

March 31
Busch Stadium, St. Louis 47,972

AVG. **.500**	RBIs **4**	BB **0**

AT-BATS			PITCHER
1st **K**	4th **2B**	5th **HR**	**Ramon Martinez** DODGERS STARTER, 4 ⅔ IP
7th **K**			

COUNT	ON BASE	OUTS
1-0	**3**	**2**

SOSA	PACE	GRIFFEY
0	**162**	**1**

FINAL: Cardinals 6, Dodgers 0

Cardinals' record: 1-0

Homer No. 1 landed in the left field seats just above Busch Stadium's visitors' bullpen.

hungry, sea-of-red sellout crowd with the fist-pumping, teammate-bumping enthusiasm of a Michael Johnson sprint to the finish line.

"People will be talking about that one for a while," said Cardinals manager Tony La Russa after a season-opening shutout that featured Todd Stottlemyre's seven-inning, three-hit pitching. A key defensive play by first baseman McGwire also was prominent, saving two runs in the fifth inning. McGwire's 10th career grand slam and his 25th home run in 52 games with the Cardinals was certainly a moment he will savor.

"It's a great feeling. How can you not acknowledge it?" he said when asked about his unusually animated curtain call. "I'm very flattered by the way (the St. Louis fans) have received me."

RUTH *The Babe's 1927 masterpiece, still considered by many the greatest home run season ever posted, began April 15 with a solo blast off Philadelphia A's righthander Howard Ehmke.*

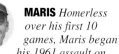

MARIS *Homerless over his first 10 games, Maris began his 1961 assault on baseball's most cherished record April 26 with a fifth-inning solo shot off Detroit righthander Paul Foytack.*

■ "McGwire is the guy. If you give him an opportunity, if you make a bad pitch to him, he's going to hurt you. With the bases loaded, we had to pitch to him. You just can't afford to put yourself in that situation." *—Dodgers manager Bill Russell*

■ "You're not going to see many people hit a ball that high and have it leave the park. I'm sure he'll say he mishit it, but he's so strong, he can miss a pitch and still do that. I can't relate, because I don't have power like that." *—Dodgers outfielder Todd Hollandsworth*

A Grand Opening

The McGwire home run show opened to rave reviews, thanks to a fifth-inning grand slam that propelled the Cardinals to victory.

Big Mac watches the flight of his first 1998 home run (right) and begins the home run trot (below) that would become an almost nightly staple for national baseball fans. The greeting at home plate (above right) and the Busch Stadium curtain call (below right) would be repeated many times over the course of a record-setting summer.

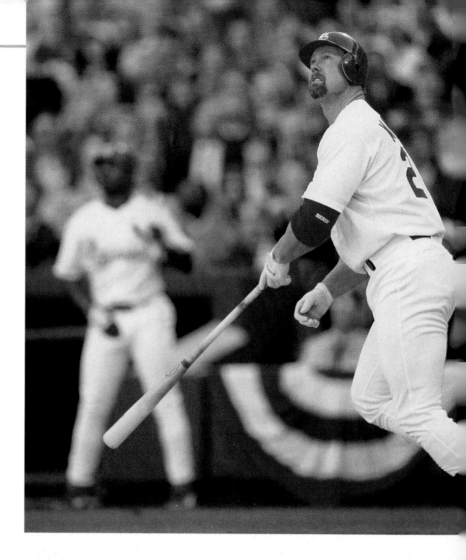

2

"To get the record, you have to average 10 home runs a month. I believe it can be done, but it has to be a perfect season."

—McGwire

Pushed by his insatiable desire for both quantity and quality, McGwire hit a dramatic 12th-inning home run into the left field seats at Busch Stadium. Big Mac's second homer in as many games, a three-run blast off rookie Frank Lankford, again provided the difference in a victory over the Los Angeles Dodgers.

Still riding the crest of his opening day grand slam,

April 2
Busch Stadium, St. Louis 27,414

AVG. .500	RBIs 7	BB 3

AT-BATS			PITCHER
1st W✓	3rd W✓	5th 1B✓	**Frank Lankford**
7th K	8th W✓	10th K	DODGERS
12th HR			RELIEVER, ⅔ IP

COUNT	ON BASE	OUTS
0-1	2	2

SOSA	PACE	GRIFFEY
0	162	1

FINAL: Cardinals 8, Dodgers 5 (12 innings)

Cardinals' record: 2-0

Homer No. 2 landed in the left field lower-deck seats at Busch Stadium.

McGwire punctuated his two-hit, three-walk Game 2 by hitting an 0-1 curveball, ending a seesaw battle that lasted more than four hours and required 14 pitchers. The Dodgers had worked a little magic of their own when pinch hitter Matt Luke singled with two out in the ninth and Thomas Howard hit a game-tying homer.

"You know anything is possible with him—is that amazing?" Cardinals manager Tony La Russa said after McGwire hit his 389th home run, tying Johnny Bench for 29th on the career list.

The homer prompted the first wave of can-you-break-the-record questions and inspired the comment that would become a regular feature of press conferences over the next five months: "If I have 50 going into September, talk to me then."

RUTH *After a non-Ruthian week, The Babe victimized the Athletics again for home run No. 2. This solo shot came off lefthander Rube Walberg in an April 23 game at Philadelphia.*

MARIS *Five more games passed before the slow-starting Maris hit his second home run—a May 3 three-run shot at Minnesota off Pedro Ramos, a righthander who would lose 20 games in 1961.*

■ "It was a lollipop curve. I knew the minute it left my hand. I can't hang a curve to him. I don't think I'll throw that pitch to him again." *—Dodgers pitcher Frank Lankford*

■ "He (Lankford) got me out (opening day) with a breaking ball, so I was looking for another. He threw me a curve and I was able to get it all." *—McGwire*

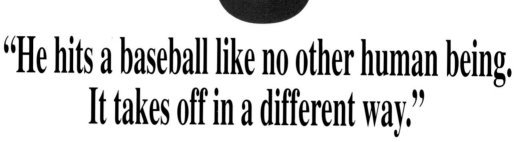

3

"He hits a baseball like no other human being. It takes off in a different way."

—Padres manager Bruce Bochy

After playing the dramatic lead for two St. Louis master-pieces, McGwire took on a sub-ordinate role in the Cardinals' first loss of the season—a 13-5 San Diego blowout at Busch Stadium. On a damp, 44-degree night made even more frigid by a six-run Padres' opening in-ning, Big Mac provided one warm moment with a two-run homer, his third in as many 1998 games.

The fifth-inning blast, which cut the Padres' lead to 9-5, landed in the left field seats, just inside the foul pole, and gave McGwire home runs in

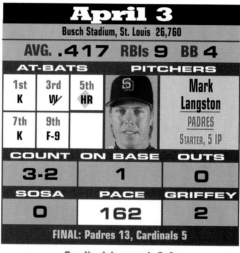

April 3
Busch Stadium, St. Louis 26,760

AVG. .417	RBIs 9	BB 4

AT-BATS			PITCHERS
1st **K**	3rd **W**	5th **HR**	**Mark Langston** PADRES STARTER, 5 IP
7th **K**	9th **F-9**		

COUNT	ON BASE	OUTS
3-2	1	0

SOSA	PACE	GRIFFEY
0	162	2

FINAL: Padres 13, Cardinals 5

Cardinals' record: 2-1

364 ft.

McGwire's third home run landed in the loge reserved level just inside the left field foul pole at Busch Stadium.

five straight games and 14 consecutive series dating to the 1997 season.

The homer was McGwire's 390th, tying him with Graig Nettles for 28th on baseball's career list.

"McGwire hit a two-run home run and it didn't really hurt us that bad," said Padres right fielder Tony Gwynn, aware of the dramatics that ac-companied Big Mac blasts in the Cardinals' season-opening victories over Los Angeles. McGwire also walked and struck out twice, finishing his third 1998 game with a major league-leading nine RBIs.

The homer, McGwire's fifth off lefthander Mark Langston in 50 career at-bats, put him on an every-other-game homer pace since his July 31, 1997 trade to St. Louis. Big Mac finished the day with 27 home runs in 54 games with the Cardinals.

 RUTH *Connecting for the second straight day, Ruth made it three home runs in 12 games with an April 24 shot off righthander Sloppy Thurston at Washington. It also was his third solo home run.*

MARIS *In his 20th game on May 6, Maris raised his unimpressive homer total to three. The fifth-inning solo blast came off Eli Grba in a game against the expansion Angels at Los Angeles.*

■ "I threw some pitches where I wanted to and some not. The one to McGwire was a changeup. I have faced him so many times, you cannot make a mistake like that or he will take advantage of that." *—Padres pitcher Mark Langston*

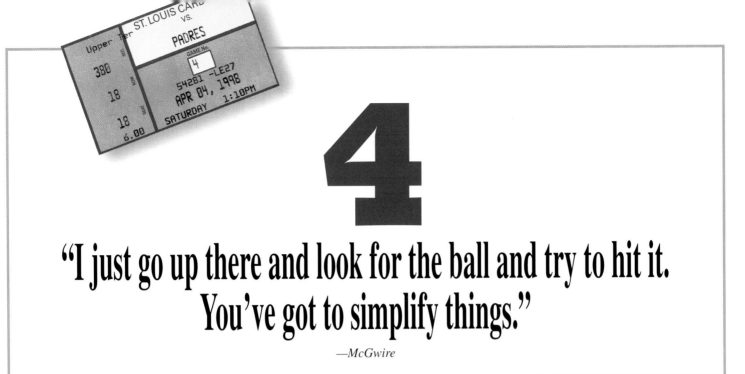

4

"I just go up there and look for the ball and try to hit it. You've got to simplify things."

—McGwire

McGwire, who pounded his way into a select power-hitting fraternity in 1997, made his first 1998 foray into exalted territory when he hit a home run in his fourth straight game, tying Willie Mays' record for consecutive homer games to begin a season.

"You put him in with Mr. Foxx and Mr. Ruth and now Mr. Mays," Cardinals manager Tony La Russa said, shaking his head. "That's serious company."

Like two of his first three homers, McGwire's shot, over the fence in left-center, was the big blow in a Cardinals' victory. It also was his first 400-foot-plus drive of the young season, a distance he soon would reach with amazing consistency. The 419-foot blast off San Diego reliever Don Wengert, a former Oakland teammate, keyed a decisive

April 4
Busch Stadium, St. Louis 34,292

AVG. **.438**   RBIs **12**   BB **5**

AT-BATS			PITCHER	
1st **K**	3rd **W**	4th **1B**		Don **Wengert**
6th **HR**	7th **6-4-3**			PADRES RELIEVER, 0 IP

COUNT	ON BASE	OUTS
2-1	**2**	**0**

SOSA	PACE	GRIFFEY
1	**162**	**3**

FINAL: Cardinals 8, Padres 6

Cardinals' record: 3-1

This shot landed near the picture of the Cardinal at the edge of the left field bleachers.

five-run sixth inning.

Big Mac's season-opening outburst, which matched the homer streak compiled by a 39-year-old Mays in 1971, was enough to convince San Diego pitching coach Dave Stewart, a McGwire teammate for seven seasons in Oakland, that the best is yet to come. "I've seen him when he was not as good," Stewart said. "I've seen him when he's been good. And now you're going to get a chance to see him when he's great."

Amazingly, all of McGwire's major league-leading 12 RBIs were the result of his four home runs.

RUTH *No. 4, Ruth's third home run in four games, came in the fifth inning of an April 29 game against his old team, the Boston Red Sox. Slim Harriss was the victim of Babe's fourth straight solo shot.*

MARIS *Slowly but surely Maris inched forward, connecting for the fourth time in a May 17 game at Yankee Stadium against Washington. Maris' first lefthanded victim was Pete Burnside.*

■ "It's unbelievable. (McGwire) has a chance to hit the ball out of the ballpark every time he walks up to the plate." —*Cardinals catcher Tom Lampkin*

■ "I'm glad to be in company with them (Mays, Foxx and Ruth). I think it's great. But it's just a day. I'm not going to sit back and dwell on what I've just done. I've got to think about what I'm going to do tomorrow." —*McGwire*

5/6/7

"He's unbelievable. No guy hits a ball like that."

——Cardinals outfielder John Mabry

All it took was some good, old-fashioned inspiration to get McGwire out of his first homerless funk of the young season. And that was provided by a 10-year-old Southern California kid who watched his dad take another giant stride in a record quest.

Matt McGwire, in from California to visit his father, spent his first night at Busch Stadium working as a batboy and watched Big Mac break an eight-game drought with three home runs against the expansion Arizona Diamondbacks.

"I tell him almost every day I talk to him that what I do in the game of baseball, I do for him," said McGwire, referring to the almost-daily phone conversations he has with his son.

But this time young Matt got a bird's-eye view of his father raking Arizona starter Jeff Suppan for third- and fifth-

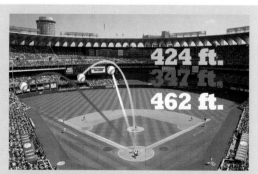

April 14		
Busch Stadium, St. Louis 31,477		
AVG. **.404**	RBIs **22**	BB **16**

AT-BATS			PITCHER
1st W/	3rd HR	5th HR	**Jeff Suppan (5&6)** STARTER, 6 IP
7th W/	8th HR		**Barry Manuel (7)** RELIEVER, ⅔ IP

COUNT	ON BASE	OUTS
1-2,1-1,2-0	1,0,1	1,2,0

SOSA	PACE	GRIFFEY
2	**87**	**6**

FINAL: Cardinals 15, Diamondbacks 5

Cardinals' record: 8-5

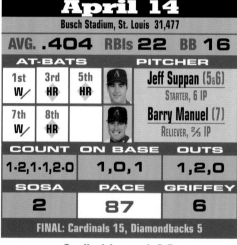

424 ft. / 347 ft. / 462 ft.

McGwire's first homer sailed over the visitors' bullpen, followed by shots off a pillar in left and near the giant Coke bottle in left center.

inning homers and connecting against Barry Manuel for a two-run, eighth-inning shot that helped the Cardinals pull away. The homers, which traveled 424, 347 and 462 feet, accounted for five RBIs. It marked Mac's third career three-homer game. Brian Jordan also homered and added four RBIs.

"The first year I played baseball in the big leagues, I played with Reggie Jackson," McGwire said. "He told me he always regretted that he never had a child who could watch him hit those 500 home runs."

The three-homer game was the first by a Cardinal since 1993, when Mark Whiten clubbed four against the Reds. It helped overcome a grand slam by Matt Williams, the first in Arizona's short history.

All of McGwire's first seven homers and 17 of his 22 RBIs came at Busch Stadium.

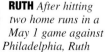

RUTH *After hitting two home runs in a May 1 game against Philadelphia, Ruth struggled through seven games before hitting his seventh homer in a May 10 game at St. Louis. The victim was Milt Gaston.*

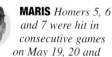

MARIS *Homers 5, 6 and 7 were hit in consecutive games on May 19, 20 and 21. Cleveland's Jim Perry and Gary Bell and Baltimore's Chuck Estrada were the victims as Maris heated up.*

■ "I'm way past the point of something Mark McGwire does that's surprising. He's a very gifted young man who's in a perfect situation for him here. He's taking advantage of it. I hope he stays healthy." —*Diamondbacks manager Buck Showalter*

■ "I guess I tried to throw too hard. The thing you have to do with him is keep the ball down out of the strike zone." —*Diamondbacks pitcher Jeff Suppan*

AS EASY AS 1-2-3: *On a McGwire-perfect night at Busch Stadium, the big first baseman hit three home runs, celebrated with 10-year-old son/batboy Matt (below center) and took several curtain calls for fans who enjoyed the Cardinals' 15-5 win over Arizona.*

Little Mac

One of the freshest faces to grace St. Louis' Busch Stadium in 1998 belonged to Matthew McGwire, the 10-year-old son of baseball's most revered slugger. Young Matt, who spent most of the time with his mother at their Southern California home, provided an inspiration that helped propel his father through several difficult stretches of his record-breaking season.

Young Matt, who enjoyed St. Louis so much during a 1997 visit that he encouraged his dad to re-sign with the Cardinals, made his major league debut as a batboy in an April 14 game against Arizona at Busch Stadium—after his father had endured an eight-game homerless drought. Not only did he perform batboy functions, he became an official greeter for Big Mac on three home runs— the first of two three-homer games McGwire would enjoy in the first seven weeks of the season.

"He's just thrilled, first, to go out on the field to shag flies," Mark McGwire said of his son after a 15-5 win over the Diamondbacks. "And he got to be batboy for the first time."

Matt would don his Cardinals uniform off and on throughout the season, every time he could hook up with his father during a St. Louis visit or a Cardinals' West Coast swing. After a July 12 game in which McGwire hit two home runs, he looked at reporters and announced, "He kissed my bat." Matt had returned to his California home just prior to the game.

Coincidence or inspiration? There's little doubt Matt's presence did have a positive effect on dad. "I just feel fortunate that he is around to see me," McGwire said. "That makes it special."

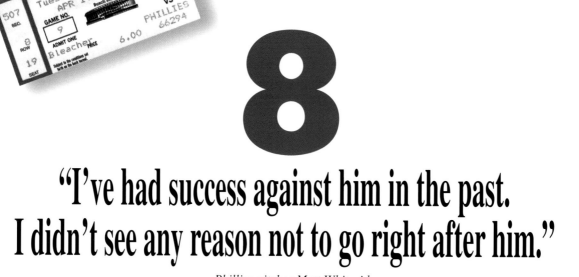

8

"I've had success against him in the past. I didn't see any reason not to go right after him."

—Phillies pitcher Matt Whiteside

McGwire continued to give love-struck St. Louis fans every reason to remain that way when he drove a fourth-inning Matt Whiteside pitch into the bleachers in left-center field. The two-run shot broke a tie and set the stage for a victory over Philadelphia. Big Mac's league-leading eighth homer also was his eighth at Busch, where he finds the inspiration almost overwhelming.

"I love playing here," McGwire said. "It's a great baseball park. (Other players) just rave about how great it is to play here. So how can you not want to play with all the energy in the stands? It's a wonderful place."

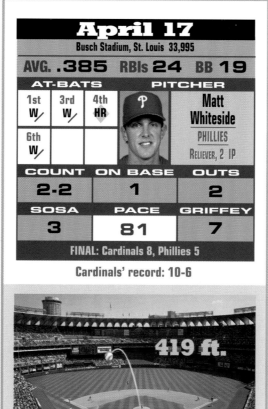

April 17
Busch Stadium, St. Louis 33,995

AVG. **.385**	RBIs **24**	BB **19**

AT-BATS		PITCHER	
1st W/	3rd W/	4th HR	**Matt Whiteside**
6th W/			PHILLIES
			Reliever, 2 IP

COUNT	ON BASE	OUTS
2-2	**1**	**2**

SOSA	PACE	GRIFFEY
3	**81**	**7**

FINAL: Cardinals 8, Phillies 5

Cardinals' record: 10-6

Homer No. 8 landed high in the left field bleachers at Busch Stadium.

The numbers through nine games at Busch Stadium seemed to support McGwire's infatuation. He had a .429 average and eight homers in 28 at-bats and had outhomered several teams, including the Phillies. Since his arrival from Oakland on July 31, 1997, McGwire had 21 homers at Busch while averaging one every 5.3 at-bats.

The blast off Whiteside came with Delino DeShields at second and first base open, a situation that invariably results in a McGwire walk. But Whiteside had enjoyed success against McGwire (2-for-13, 0 homers) in his American League days and decided to take his chances.

One inning later, Ron Gant broke another tie with a three-run, pinch-hit homer that traveled 420 feet—1 foot longer than McGwire's.

RUTH *The Babe's eighth homer is a trivia footnote. The May 11 blast came off St. Louis Browns righthander Ernie Nevers, who went on to Hall of Fame glory—in the National Football League.*

MARIS *Picking up the pace, Maris connected for the fifth time in an eight-day span, this time off Boston righthander Gene Conley. The two-run homer was hit in the Yankees' 35th game.*

■ "I was looking just to drive it up the middle. It was a good pitch and I just got enough to get it out." *—McGwire*

■ "They need to start changing the measurement system for him. Using feet is getting too ridiculous. Quarter-miles would be good." *—Phillies outfielder Doug Glanville*

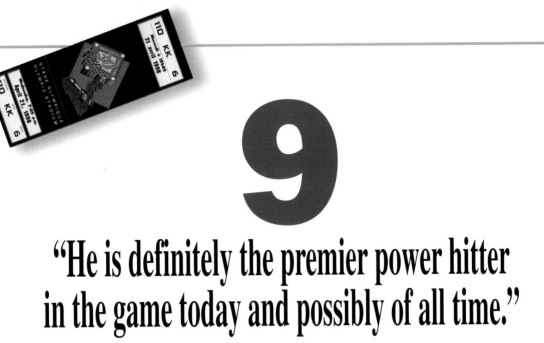

9

"He is definitely the premier power hitter in the game today and possibly of all time."

—Cardinals pitcher Todd Stottlemyre

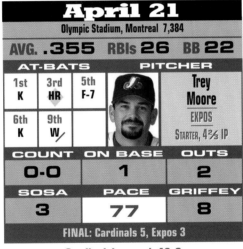

April 21
Olympic Stadium, Montreal 7,384

AVG. .355	RBIs 26	BB 22

AT-BATS			PITCHER	
1st K	3rd HR	5th F-7		Trey Moore
6th K	9th W			EXPOS STARTER, 4⅔ IP

COUNT	ON BASE	OUTS
0-0	1	2

SOSA	PACE	GRIFFEY
3	77	8

FINAL: Cardinals 5, Expos 3

Cardinals' record: 13-6

The long home run landed in the open area to the right of the seats in Olympic Stadium's left center field.

The McGwire home run show played to quiet reviews in Montreal, where only 7,384 fans were in attendance. But those who did find their way to Olympic Stadium were rewarded with a third-inning Big Mac bomb that traveled 437 feet to left-center field, giving the Cardinals a 2-0 lead.

McGwire's two-out shot off Montreal lefthander Trey Moore was his first road homer of the season and his first ever at Olympic Stadium. It also was his fifth of 400 or more feet and second-longest of the season.

"'Pops' used to say that Mantle hit the ball as far as anybody he's ever seen," said Cardinals starter and winning pitcher Todd Stottlemyre, referring to his father, former New York Yankees pitcher Mel Stottlemyre. "But I would say that Mac would put up a great argument. If somebody can hit the ball farther than Mac, I'd like to have seen him play."

Nobody could top McGwire for distance against the Expos, but teammate Ron Gant upstaged him for the second time in a week with a 414-foot homer that broke a 3-3 tie and lifted the Cardinals to a 5-3 victory.

It was Gant's third home run of the season and his third in games in which McGwire had also homered—all Cardinals' victories.

 RUTH *The Babe waits until the eighth inning to contribute a solo home run in the Yankees' 9-2 victory over Detroit on May 17 at Navin Field. The victim was righthander Rip Collins.*

 MARIS *His eighth homer in May began a long hot streak that would carry him into record contention. Chicago's Cal McLish served up Maris' ninth homer in a May 28 game at New York.*

■ "You can't hit a home run every at-bat every game. It just doesn't happen. But nobody ever writes that. They write how easy it is. That's what the national press is doing. But I like to do other things besides hitting a home run." —*McGwire*

10

"I don't know what the pitch was. I was looking for anything."

—McGwire

What happens when a fastball from a 6-7, 240-pounder meets a 6-5, 250-pound swing? In the case of Philadelphia pitcher Jerry Spradlin vs. Mark McGwire, the answer was predictable—a monster 419-foot drive over the center-field fence that capped a six-run, game-deciding rally in a victory over the Phillies.

McGwire's second road home run and his first ever at Veterans Stadium was a two-run shot that wiped out a 5-4 Phillies lead. It came off a big righthander Big Mac doesn't face with enthusiasm. "When you're that big, and

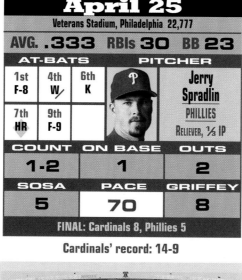

April 25
Veterans Stadium, Philadelphia 22,777

AVG. .333	RBIs 30	BB 23

AT-BATS			PITCHER
1st F-8	4th W	6th K	Jerry Spradlin PHILLIES Reliever, ⅓ IP
7th HR	9th F-9		

COUNT	ON BASE	OUTS
1-2	1	2

SOSA	PACE	GRIFFEY
5	70	8

FINAL: Cardinals 8, Phillies 5

Cardinals' record: 14-9

419 ft.

The ball hit the black tarp hanging in center field at Philadelphia's Veterans Stadium.

those arms and legs," McGwire said with a shake of his head. "He throws very, very hard. ... He's very tough."

McGwire, who had been homerless in 15 career at-bats at Veterans Stadium, put on quite a show for the enthusiastic Phillies fans. First he hit the ball out of the park on 20 batting-practice swings, including four drives into the upper deck. Then he provided the decisive blow during the game.

Veterans Stadium was the 28th park in which McGwire had homered, leaving Atlanta's Turner Field and New York's Shea Stadium as the only parks in which he had played without going deep.

Before the six-run seventh, Phillies starter Matt Beech, a lefthander with a career 5.58 ERA, had shut out the Cardinals on one hit.

RUTH *The methodical pace continued as Ruth connected for the 10th time, in a May 22 contest at Cleveland. The sixth-inning home run off righthander Benn Karr accounted for two Yankee runs.*

MARIS *Nearing the end of May with a bang, Maris touched off two home runs, his 10th and 11th, against Boston righthanders Gene Conley and Mike Fornieles on May 30 in a game at Fenway Park.*

■ "(The pitch) was not where I wanted it. You'd almost be surprised if he didn't hit it out." —*Phillies pitcher Jerry Spradlin*

■ "You can never be satisfied." —*McGwire, on why he took extra batting practice after the game*

53

11

"Not only is he a great player, but he's so humble. He's a gentle giant. He just takes all the hoopla in stride."

—Cubs first baseman Mark Grace

McGwire was obscured for seven innings by hard-throwing Chicago rookie Kerry Wood and a thick fog that enveloped Wrigley Field after a two-hour rain delay. But the fourth pitch from Cubs reliever Marc Pisciotta in the eighth became another notch for McGwire's growing reputation as the greatest pure power hitter since the days of Babe Ruth.

McGwire struck out twice and flied out once against the mid-90s deliveries of the 20-year-old Wood, who

April 30
Wrigley Field, Chicago 24,210

AVG. .318	RBIs 36	BB 27

AT-BATS			PITCHER	
1st K	4th K	6th F-9		Marc Pisciotta
8th HR				CUBS Reliever, ⅓ IP

COUNT	ON BASE	OUTS
2-1	1	1

SOSA	PACE	GRIFFEY
6	66	11

FINAL: Cubs 8, Cardinals 3

Cardinals' record: 16-11

371 ft.

In a heavy Wrigley fog, McGwire hit a homer into the left center field bleachers, just in front of the chain-link fence behind the stands.

allowed only five hits and one run over seven innings. It didn't take long for McGwire to catch up with reliever Pisciotta, but his two-run, 371-foot drive over the left field wall was too little, too late.

McGwire's line drive literally disappeared into a fog that had thickened so much by the eighth inning that left fielder Henry Rodriguez could not pick the ball up and never left his position. Cardinals third baseman Gary Gaetti marveled at Rodriguez's predicament: "McGwire's ball, it could've hit him right in the face. The fog made it hard to play, but both teams had to do it."

Wood, who had been roughed up in his previous start against the Dodgers, attacked McGwire like a seasoned veteran. "I've got a lot of respect for him," Wood said, "but I didn't put too much emphasis on just him."

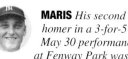

RUTH *Senators righthander Sloppy Thurston made his second appearance on Ruth's home run ledger in a May 23 game at Washington. Ruth's solo blast came in the Yankees' 34th game.*

MARIS *His second homer in a 3-for-5 May 30 performance at Fenway Park was a three-run blast off Mike Fornieles in the eighth inning. His 10th and 11th homers came in the Yankees' 40th game.*

■ "Nobody hits the ball that far with an easy swing like he does. He has a short, easy swing and he's not trying to hit the ball out of the park." —Cubs coach Billy Williams

12

"He's a modern-day Babe Ruth. I have the ultimate respect for him. Everyone does."

—Cubs relief ace Rod Beck

Leave it to Chicago relief ace Rod Beck to put things in perspective after surrendering a two-run, ninth-inning home run to McGwire before closing out a 6-5 Cubs' victory.

"He gets paid to hit home runs and I get paid to save ballgames," Beck said. "We both did our jobs today."

Beck was more adventurous than his Chicago comrades, who pitched around the Cardinals' first baseman and the major league RBI leader (38), walking him three times as the Cubs built their lead.

Through 28 games, the ever-patient McGwire drew 30 bases on balls—putting him on a pace to break Babe Ruth's single-season walk record of 170—and compiled an impressive .484 on-base percentage. Such numbers might help the team's overall offensive production, but they were not

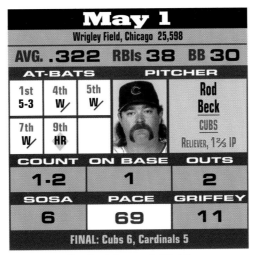

May 1

Wrigley Field, Chicago 25,598

AVG. .322	RBIs 38	BB 30

AT-BATS		PITCHER

1st 5-3	4th W	5th W
7th W	9th HR	

Rod Beck
CUBS
Reliever, 1⅔ IP

COUNT	ON BASE	OUTS
1-2	1	2

SOSA	PACE	GRIFFEY
6	69	11

FINAL: Cubs 6, Cardinals 5

Cardinals' record: 16-12

362 ft.

This towering shot landed in the left center field bleachers at Wrigley Field, just in front of the chain-link fence behind the stands.

winning the favor of fans who pay to see him swing the bat.

"People don't want to see him walk," Cubs left fielder Henry Rodriguez admitted. "They want to see him swing. He's the King Kong of baseball."

McGwire's 362-foot drive into Wrigley Field's left field seats was the 399th home run of his career, leaving him one short of an exclusive club that includes only 25 other men. Even more exclusive was a Cardinals' 400-homer club that included only one player—Hall of Famer Stan Musial (475).

RUTH *The Babe continued his early Sloppy Thurston assault with a three-run shot in a May 28 doubleheader opener against Washington. Of his 12 homers, three had come off Thurston.*

MARIS *The Yankee right fielder hit his third home run against the Red Sox in two days—a bases-empty, third-inning shot off righthander Billy Muffett in a May 31 game at Fenway Park.*

■ "I'm sure it will be special when it happens." *—McGwire, looking forward to his 400th career home run*

■ "Ray's the first guy who's ever protected me (in the lineup) my whole career. I never had anybody protect me in Oakland. I was always protecting them." *—McGwire, on Cardinals' cleanup hitter Ray Lankford*

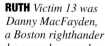

13

"When people put my name next to Ruth's name, it still blows me away. I'm still in awe."

—McGwire

400!

McGwire carved his first major notch into the 1998 record books with a towering drive that stood up to a strong New York wind and settled into the left field seats, a paltry 358 feet from home plate and just inside the foul pole. What the home run lacked in distance and artistic merit it more than made up for with height and drama.

"I'm still not sure that ball ever came down," said Rick Reed, the Mets righthander who served up McGwire's milestone home run. "Anywhere you throw it, it's in his power."

McGwire's two-run blast, his first home run at Shea Stadium, came in the third inning with the Cardinals trailing 1-0. The ball appeared to be headed for straightaway left field, but the wind blew it toward the left

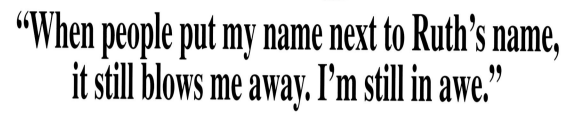

May 8

Shea Stadium, New York 16,132

AVG. .311	RBIs 40	BB 40

AT-BATS · PITCHER

1st W✓	3rd HR	5th F-3	Rick Reed
8th K			METS
			STARTER, 7 IP

COUNT	ON BASE	OUTS
0-2	1	1

SOSA	PACE	GRIFFEY
7	62	14

FINAL: Mets 9, Cardinals 2

Cardinals' record: 17-17

The ball landed in the seats just inside the left field foul pole at Shea Stadium.

field corner and McGwire stopped at the first base bag before getting umpire Sam Holbrook's home run signal. Big Mac's league-leading 39th and 40th RBIs were all the offense the Cardinals could muster in an otherwise disappointing loss to the Mets.

McGwire became the 26th player to reach the 400 plateau but the first to get there in fewer at-bats than Babe Ruth. McGwire achieved his milestone on at-bat No. 4,726, 128 fewer than The Bambino needed. No other player reached 400 home runs in fewer than 5,300 at-bats.

Shea Stadium became the 29th park in which McGwire had homered. That left only Turner Field, the Astrodome, Dodger Stadium, Cinergy Field and Bank One Ballpark on his N.L. hit list. McGwire had yet to play in the latter four parks.

RUTH *Victim 13 was Danny MacFayden, a Boston righthander who served up a solo shot in the eighth inning of a May 29 game at Yankee Stadium. It was Ruth's second homer in as many days.*

MARIS *A heavy June home run barrage began on June 2 when Maris connected with two men on base in a game at Chicago. Maris' 13th homer was his second off White Sox righthander Cal McLish.*

■ "I don't know. I don't play the game for records. I play the game because I love it. It just happens to be a milestone." —*McGwire, on the significance of career homer No. 400*

■ "I knew I hit it well, but I didn't know if the wind was going to bring it back. It was howling. The flag was blowing straight in. When the ball left the infield, it looked as if it was dead left and it ended up over by the pole." —*McGwire*

McMILESTONE: *It was a 400th-homer-type of day at New York's Shea Stadium, where McGwire took his first giant step in his march toward baseball immortality.*

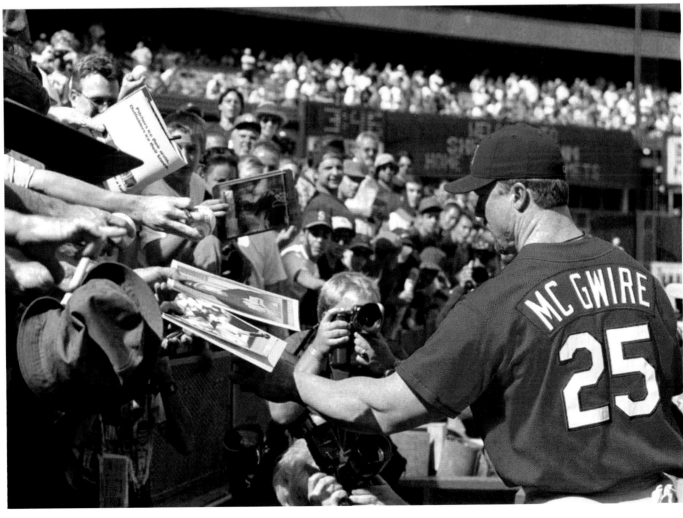

ST. LOUIS CARDINALS vs. BREWERS

GAME No. 16

Upper
326
20
11
6.00

L15258 -LE19
MAY 12, 1998 7:10PM
TUESDAY

14

"If that one didn't get stopped by the bleachers, it probably would have gone in the river."

—Cardinals teammate John Mabry

McGwire, going where no man had gone before, sent a special-delivery missile that was retrieved by a young fan in the upper deck at Busch Stadium—the longest blow ever launched by a Cardinal or a visitor in the 32-year history of the St. Louis ballpark.

McGwire's fifth-inning, three-run blast traveled 527 feet to left-center and cleared the main scoreboard. Not only did the titanic blow stun the crowd of 25,680, it wiped out a 3-1 St. Louis deficit in a game the Cardinals would win in extra innings. The blow came off Milwaukee starter Paul Wagner, after Royce Clayton had singled and Ray Lankford had walked.

"I went to the well too many times with my fastball," Wagner said. "For him to hit it 550 feet, he must have guessed right. It was a great time for the

slider, but I stayed with the fastball."

McGwire's home run would have been another in his growing line of game-winners, but Milwaukee's Jeff Cirillo hit a two-run, ninth-inning homer that forced extra innings. A Delino DeShields 10th-inning single finally decided the issue.

The previous measured Busch Stadium distance record had been set in September 1997 by McGwire, on the memorable St. Louis day when he signed a three-year contract and then drove a pitch from Los Angeles righthander Ramon Martinez 517 feet in his first at-bat.

But Brewers manager Phil Garner remembered a Busch Stadium home run hit by Willie Stargell when they were Pittsburgh teammates.

"Those two (Mac's and Stargell's) are in another category," Garner said.

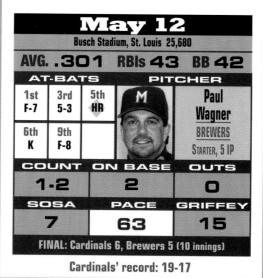

May 12		
Busch Stadium, St. Louis 25,680		
AVG. .301	RBIs 43	BB 42

AT-BATS			PITCHER
1st F-7	3rd 5-3	5th HR	Paul Wagner
6th K	9th F-8		BREWERS STARTER, 5 IP

COUNT	ON BASE	OUTS
1-2	2	0

SOSA	PACE	GRIFFEY
7	63	15

FINAL: Cardinals 6, Brewers 5 (10 innings)

Cardinals' record: 19-17

527 ft.

The longest measured home run at Busch Stadium landed in the upper deck in left center.

RUTH *The Bambino delivered in the 11th inning of a May 30 doubleheader nightcap at Philadelphia. The solo blast off lefty Rube Walberg, Ruth's 14th, gave the Yankees a 6-5 victory.*

MARIS *Roger's 14th homer, his second three-run blast in as many days against the White Sox, came at the expense of righthander Bob Shaw in a June 3 game at Chicago's Comiskey Park.*

■ "He has the power of three men. I've never faced anybody like him. He's a man among boys." —*Milwaukee pitcher Paul Wagner*

■ "It excites the people, but I have to look at it as one at-bat. I can't sit there and say, 'OK, great.' I have to worry about the next at-bat and worry about tomorrow." —*McGwire*

A LONG STORY: *Brewers righthander Paul Wagner fired and McGwire delivered—a mammoth 527-foot message to pitchers throughout the National League.*

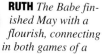

15

"I don't manage (McGwire). I just tell him what time the game is and who we're playing."

—Cardinals manager Tony La Russa

The focus of this game was on home runs, but not of the McGwire ilk. Atlanta Braves followers would have been satisfied with just one, measly 330-footer over the left field fence—a garden variety shot that would have enabled their team to establish a record (26) for consecutive games with at least one homer.

They didn't get it. But they were treated to an atypical home run by McGwire en route to a victory over the Cardinals.

"If we had hit a home run and lost, everybody would be dejected," Braves third baseman Chipper Jones said. "Tonight, being dominated for

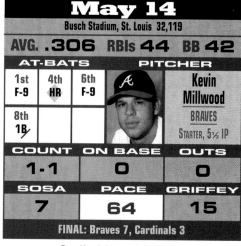

May 14
Busch Stadium, St. Louis 32,119

AVG. .306	RBIs 44	BB 42

AT-BATS			PITCHER
1st F-9	4th HR	6th F-9	Kevin Millwood
8th 1B			BRAVES
			STARTER, 5⅓ IP

COUNT	ON BASE	OUTS
1-1	0	0

SOSA	PACE	GRIFFEY
7	64	15

FINAL: Braves 7, Cardinals 3

Cardinals' record: 19-19

381 ft.

This unusual McGwire home run sailed into the Cardinals' bullpen—in right center.

seven innings, it was just nice to come back and win."

The Cardinals carried a 3-0 lead into the Braves' eighth, thanks in part to McGwire's fourth-inning home run—a 381-foot fly ball off Kevin Millwood that carried into the Cardinals' bullpen in right-center. It was Big Mac's first home run to the right of center field, and it gave him 23 homers in 41 career games at Busch Stadium.

Mark Petkovsek held the Braves to five hits through seven innings, but they broke through for seven eighth-inning runs against the Cardinals bullpen, winning for the 15th time in 17 games.

McGwire, who had captured national attention with his bat, showed a different side of his game in the fifth inning when he made two good plays on tricky grounders.

 RUTH *The Babe finished May with a flourish, connecting in both games of a month-ending doubleheader at Philadelphia. Ruth's first-game, two-run shot, No. 15, was hit off righthander Jack Quinn.*

MARIS *After hitting his seventh homer in an eight-day span, Maris was on a roll. No. 15 was his third in as many games against the White Sox. The victim was Russ Kemmerer in a June 4 game at Chicago.*

■ "All of my success is due to hard work. I study pitchers. I spend extra time in the cage. It's an everyday process and it's made me a better, more experienced hitter. Hard work pays off. It gives me a better chance to succeed. I know that there is always someone behind you working harder, so that's what has kept me driven." *—McGwire*

16

"They (McGwire homers) disappear and get real small, real quick. It's fortunate they only count as one run."

—Marlins manager Jim Leyland

The ball shot off his bat and soared toward the center field backdrop at Busch Stadium, instantly energizing the 41,464 fans who had hoped to witness another McGwire home run. The cheers reverberated through the stadium, and every body in every corner of the house rose in unison, straining to track an unfamiliar flight pattern.

As the ball rose up, up and away toward uncharted territory, so did the noisy din that enveloped the stadium. Ecstasy turned to disbelief when the ball, finally on a downward trajectory, banged high off the Post-Dispatch sign, just below the luxury boxes and

May 16
Busch Stadium, St. Louis 41,464

AVG. .310	RBIs 45	BB 46

AT-BATS		PITCHER
1st K	4th HR	5th W
7th F-3		Livan Hernandez MARLINS Starter, 6 IP

COUNT	ON BASE	OUTS
1-0	0	0

SOSA	PACE	GRIFFEY
8	65	15

FINAL: Cardinals 5, Marlins 4

Cardinals' record: 20-20

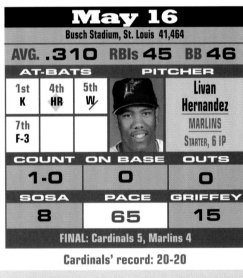

545 ft.

McGwire broke his own home run distance mark at Busch with a shot off a sign in center field. He had set the previous record four days earlier.

upper-deck seats that had always provided safe haven from guided missiles. Distance from home plate: 545 feet.

"It's the best ball I've ever hit," a stoic McGwire said after his team's victory over the Florida Marlins. "I don't think I can hit one better than that."

The home run, a solo shot off of 1997 World Series Most Valuable Player Livan Hernandez, was the longest drive ever measured at Busch Stadium. It was 18 feet longer than the 527-footer McGwire had stroked four days earlier against Milwaukee and 7 feet longer than his longest career blast—a 1997 homer off Seattle's Randy Johnson.

McGwire tied Colorado's Vinny Castilla for the major league homer lead, but teammate Brian Jordan secured the victory with a tie-breaking, seventh-inning homer.

RUTH *Home run No. 16 off Howard Ehmke in the second game of a May 31 doubleheader gives Ruth 11 home runs on the road. The Babe's 16 homers have been hit through 43 Yankee games.*

MARIS *A three-run homer off Minnesota righthander Ed Palmquist punctuates a four-RBI day in a June 6 game at Yankee Stadium. Maris' 16th comes in New York's 48th game.*

■ "I saw people in the upper deck ducking. You'd think a guy who has hit his longest home run would pull it. But this was to straight-away center. If he ever pulls one—and this is completely absurd—he may hit one out of the park." *—Marlins coach Rich Donnelly*

■ "If I stood at home ... and you said somebody was going to hit one in the center field upper deck, I'd have said, 'No way.' Well, I was right. He missed—by 6 inches." *—Cardinals catcher Tom Pagnozzi*

OUCH MARKS THE SPOT: *An oversized Band-Aid covers the dent on the center field sign off which McGwire bounced the longest recorded home run in Busch Stadium history. The shot off Florida's Livan Hernandez traveled 545 feet.*

ou in. S

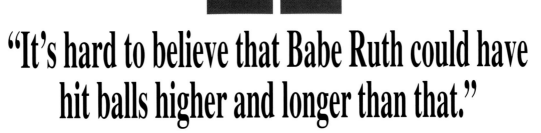

17

"It's hard to believe that Babe Ruth could have hit balls higher and longer than that."

—Marlins catcher Mike Piazza

It was a case of inopportune timing.

Florida's Jesus Sanchez stopped the Cardinals on five hits over 7⅓ innings for his third win of the season, but he couldn't navigate around another gargantuan McGwire home run.

McGwire, in the midst of a stretch in which he would hit 16 homers in May, connected with the bases empty in the fourth inning—his fifth homer in nine games.

The towering drive to left hit the green facing in the upper deck at Busch Stadium, 478 feet from the plate. His 17th homer paled in comparison to the 527- and 545-foot shots he had recorded over the previous six-day span.

"I think you're seeing the guy that's probably the best power hitter in the history of the game," marveled Marlins

May 18
Busch Stadium, St. Louis 36,820

AVG. .301	RBIs 46	BB 48

AT-BATS			PITCHER
1st F-8	4th HR	6th F-9	**Jesus Sanchez** MARLINS STARTER, 7⅓ IP
8th F-9			

COUNT	ON BASE	OUTS
2-0	0	0

SOSA	PACE	GRIFFEY
8	66	16

FINAL: Marlins 7, Cardinals 3

Cardinals' record: 21-21

478 ft.

McGwire drove his 17th homer into the upper deck in left field at Busch Stadium.

catcher Mike Piazza. "I'm known to have hit some home runs myself, but never anything like the way he does it. I'm not even close to him. When you hear the sound as it comes off the bat, you can't believe it."

Piazza had a bird's-eye view of McGwire's memorable 517-foot shot off then-Los Angeles teammate Ramon Martinez in September 1997. Then he watched McGwire beat the Dodgers with an opening day grand slam and a 12th-inning, second-day homer to open the 1998 season. The 545- and 478-footers came after his trade to the Marlins.

Sanchez, however, got the last laugh, retiring McGwire twice. "It's good to see young pitchers like that, when they're real aggressive and go at hitters," McGwire said of the Marlins starter. "He doesn't mess around."

RUTH *Earl Whitehill of Detroit joined Rube Walberg as the only lefthanders to give up home runs to Ruth. Whitehill became a member of Babe's hit list in a June 5 game at Yankee Stadium.*

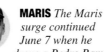

MARIS *The Maris surge continued June 7 when he drove a Pedro Ramos pitch over the Yankee Stadium fence for his second three-run homer in two days against the Minnesota Twins.*

■ "It was like a batting-practice fastball. I got good extension on it." —McGwire

■ "My kids play Babe Ruth League. In 15 years, it will be the Big Mac League. And a home run, from now on, shouldn't be a dinger or a bomb. It should just be a Mac." —*Marlins coach Rich Donnelly*

■ "To me, that's just a high line drive." —*Cardinals manager Tony La Russa*

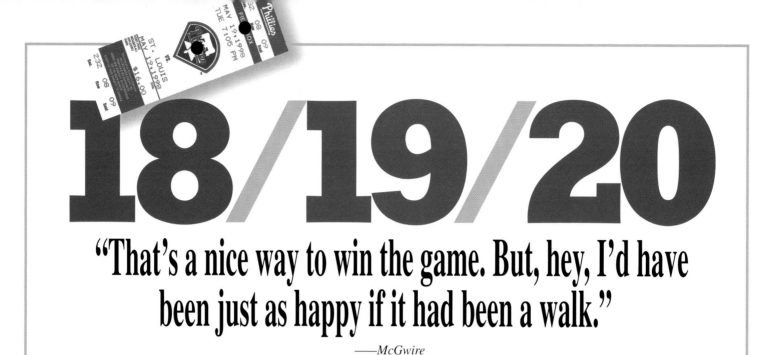

18/19/20

"That's a nice way to win the game. But, hey, I'd have been just as happy if it had been a walk."

——McGwire

Big Mac took his batting-practice show to Philadelphia and then extended it into the game. When he was finished, the Cardinals first baseman had added three home runs and 1,362 feet to his ever-growing ledger.

McGwire's latest explosion was enough to ensure a Cardinals' victory—but just barely. The third of three tape-measure, two-run homers came in the eighth inning and provided the game-winning margin.

"I think he's only hit one this year where the game wasn't close," Cardinals manager Tony La Russa said. "He keeps hitting them in game situations."

Homer No. 1 was served up by Phillies starter Tyler Green and keyed a three-run Cardinals' third inning.

The 440-footer, which sailed over the fence in center field, was the baby of

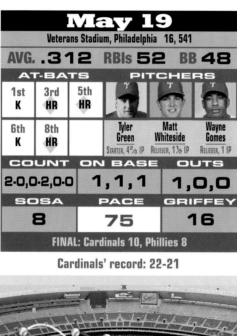

May 19		
Veterans Stadium, Philadelphia 16, 541		
AVG. .312	RBIs 52	BB 48

AT-BATS

1st K	3rd HR	5th HR
6th K	8th HR	

PITCHERS

Tyler Green	Matt Whiteside	Wayne Gomes
Starter, 4⅔ IP	Reliever, 1⅓ IP	Reliever, 1 IP

COUNT	ON BASE	OUTS
2-0,0-2,0-0	1, 1, 1	1, 0, 0

SOSA	PACE	GRIFFEY
8	75	16

FINAL: Cardinals 10, Phillies 8

Cardinals' record: 22-21

Homer No. 1 landed above the black tarp in center field; No. 2 hit the upper-deck facade; and No. 3 reached the upper deck.

Big Mac's trifecta.

McGwire's second two-run homer came in the fifth and helped the Cardinals build a five-run lead. This 471-foot bomb to center exploded in the face of reliever Matt Whiteside.

But the ultimate touch came in the eighth when McGwire sent a moonshot 451 feet into the left field upper deck on the first pitch from Wayne Gomes.

McGwire was saluted with standing ovations from the modest Veterans Stadium crowd and by his pitching victims afterward.

"Whether you're a Phillies fan or a Cardinals fan, you have to applaud the guy," Gomes said.

The outburst gave McGwire five home runs in four games and seven in eight. He became the 12th player in history to record two three-homer games in the same season.

 RUTH *After hitting his 18th home run in a June 7 game against the Chicago White Sox, Ruth belted two more off Cleveland lefthander Garland Buckeye four days later at Yankee Stadium.*

 MARIS *No. 18 on June 9 was followed on June 11 by Maris' second multihomer game—off Eli Grba and Johnny James at Yankee Stadium—two of the four he would hit against the expansion Angels.*

■ "He's a special player. What he did here tonight, he just kind of took it into his own hands." *—Phillies manager Terry Francona*

■ "If I came to see Mark McGwire and was sitting in the upper deck and he hit three home runs 450 feet, I might be cheering, too. I might have said, 'Wow.' " *—Phillies pitcher Wayne Gomes*

TRIFECTA: *Visions of another McGwire three-homer assault, the final of which left Philadelphia righthander Wayne Gomes (left) in a disconsolate mood. It was vintage McGwire: All three homers measured more than 400 feet.*

21

"I've never had (a Big Mac sandwich) in my whole life. ... I don't like that special sauce and all the other stuff."

—McGwire

Beanie Babies, Big Macs and a victory. McGwire's 21st home run, into the upper deck at Busch Stadium, helped complete a mammoth haul of rewards for the 47,549 fans who witnessed it.

McGwire's sixth-inning blast off righthander Mark Gardner, a two-run shot that gave the Cardinals a 2-1 lead over San Francisco on Beanie Babies night, landed in upper-deck Section 383, 425 feet from home plate.

That section is labeled "Big Mac Land" under terms of a McDonald's restaurant promotion that offers free Big Mac sandwiches to every person producing a ticket stub for a game in which McGwire homers into the specified area.

"It was a long game," said left fielder Ron Gant after delivering a game-winning single off Giants closer Robb Nen in

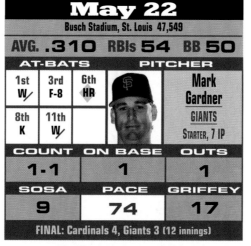

May 22
Busch Stadium, St. Louis 47,549

AVG. .310	RBIs 54	BB 50

AT-BATS — **PITCHER**

1st W/	3rd F-8	6th HR
8th K	11th W/	

Mark Gardner
GIANTS
STARTER, 7 IP

COUNT	ON BASE	OUTS
1-1	1	1

SOSA	PACE	GRIFFEY
9	74	17

FINAL: Cardinals 4, Giants 3 (12 innings)

Cardinals' record: 24-22

425 ft.

McGwire crushed one into Big Mac Land, located in Busch Stadium's left field upper deck.

the 12th inning. "I'm kind of looking forward to one of those Big Macs."

The 425-foot drive was the shortest of McGwire's last six home runs and measured 3 feet shorter than the eighth-inning home run hit by teammate Ray Lankford. McGwire entered the game averaging a major league-best 421 feet per homer, and each of his previous five had traveled 440 feet or longer.

McGwire's major league-leading 21st homer would have been the game-winner if not for a dramatic two-run, ninth-inning home run by Giants' pinch hitter Bill Mueller off Cardinals reliever Jeff Brantley.

Mueller's drive, which followed a Barry Bonds double, tied the game and forced extra innings. It was Brantley's second blown save in nine opportunities.

RUTH *Three homers in two days: Ruth's latest victim was Cleveland righthander George Uhle in a June 12 game at Yankee Stadium. That gave him 21 home runs in 53 Yankee games.*

MARIS *The torrid pace continued when Maris pounded his 21st homer and his ninth in the first 13 days of June—a solo shot at Cleveland against tough righthander Jim Perry.*

■ "That was probably a short (home run) for him. I think he's locked in and he's guessing right and seeing the ball good. I don't know if it's going to last all year, but he's swinging the bat real well." *—Giants pitcher Mark Gardner*

HAMBURGER HEAVEN: *When McGwire hit Big Mac Land with a 425-foot drive against the Giants, he gave ecstatic Busch Stadium fans something to sink their teeth into.*

22/23

"At least I made *SportsCenter.*"

—Giants pitcher Rich Rodriguez

After watching McGwire pound three home runs and lead the Cardinals past his Giants in consecutive games, San Francisco manager Dusty Baker came to a logical conclusion. "He hits the ball farther than anyone I've ever seen," Baker said.

Actually, McGwire's first home run, a bases-empty shot in the fourth inning off left-hander Rich Rodriguez, was a mini-blast by Big Mac standards—a 366-foot line drive that rocketed over the left field wall. But No. 2, a three-run homer in the fifth, was the stuff of which highlights are made. The drive off John Johnstone banged off the scoreboard in left-center, 477 feet from the plate.

The multihomer game was McGwire's third of the season and 45th of his career. And the four RBIs raised his league-

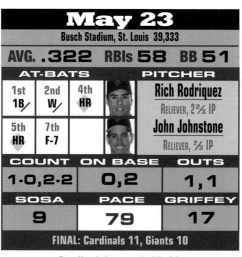

May 23
Busch Stadium, St. Louis 39,333

AVG. **.322**	RBIs **58**	BB **51**

AT-BATS | **PITCHER**

1st 1B/	2nd W/	4th HR	**Rich Rodriguez** RELIEVER, 2⅔ IP
5th HR	7th F-7		**John Johnstone** RELIEVER, ⅔ IP

COUNT	ON BASE	OUTS
1-0, 2-2	0, 2	1, 1

SOSA	PACE	GRIFFEY
9	79	17

FINAL: Cardinals 11, Giants 10

Cardinals' record: 25-22

366 ft.

McGwire's first homer landed in the loge reserved level in left field at Busch; his second bounced off the sign on the left field scoreboard.

leading count to 58. With 11 home runs in his last 13 games, he was on pace for an unlikely 79. The two home runs brought his Busch Stadium count to an almost unbelievable 28 in 47 games.

But of more importance to McGwire was the timing of his second blast, which broke an 8-8 tie and allowed the Cardinals to post a one-run victory. He was quick to point out that his battle with Johnstone was not as easy as it might have appeared.

"He made some good pitches on me," McGwire said. "I'm sitting behind in the count and I just reacted well to his slider."

The result was his seventh home run of 450 or more feet this season and his 14th over 400 feet. Two unbelievable shots topped the magical 500-foot barrier.

RUTH *Babe hit No. 22 off St. Louis lefty Tom Zachary, a name that would become prominent in his record season. But it took almost a week before he hit 23 and 24 in a June 22 doubleheader against Boston.*

MARIS *After a three-game drought, Maris started another hot streak with his 23rd home run—a bases-empty shot off Detroit lefthander Don Mossi in a June 17 game at Tiger Stadium.*

■ "I knew it was gone the minute I let it go. It was a slider that was too high." *—Giants pitcher John Johnstone*

■ "When I'm at the plate, I'm mentally locked in. This is a thinking-man's game. I don't care what anybody says. You've got to be able to use your mind. Sometimes you think right and sometimes you think wrong. But if you think wrong, you make adjustments." *—McGwire*

GIANT STRIDES: *Cardinals Brian Jordan (bottom left) and Ray Lankford (below left) provided fist-bumping partners after two more McGwire home runs—his second and third in two games against San Francisco.*

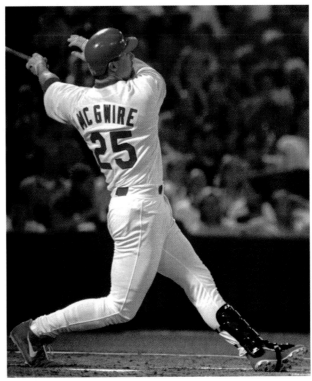

MARATHON MEN: *McGwire provided the dramatics with a 12th-inning equalizer against Robb Nen, but the Giants (above) got the last laugh in the 17th inning.*

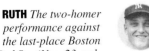

24

"Walk him. He's so locked in right now."

—Giants left fielder Barry Bonds when asked how to pitch to McGwire

When you're hot, you're hot. And not even a 98-mph Robb Nen fastball or the heavy shadows engulfing the home plate area at Busch Stadium could keep McGwire from his appointed rounds.

Big Mac, who had struck out with the bases loaded against San Francisco closer Nen in the 10th inning, was down to his final strike in the 12th when he sent a 397-foot drive into the left field seats for a two-run homer. That retied a game the Cardinals eventually would lose in the 17th.

McGwire's latest dramatic blast was set up by a Barry Bonds home run that tied the game in the ninth inning and a two-run homer by San Francisco second baseman Jeff Kent in the top of the 12th.

"None of us in the infield or outfield moved," left fielder Bonds said, referring to

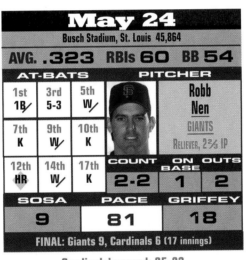

May 24		
Busch Stadium, St. Louis 45,864		
AVG. **.323**	RBIs **60**	BB **54**

AT-BATS			**PITCHER**	
1st **1B**	3rd **5-3**	5th **W**		**Robb Nen**
7th **K**	9th **W**	10th **K**		**GIANTS**
12th **HR**	14th **W**	17th **K**		Reliever, 2⅔ IP

	COUNT	ON BASE	OUTS
	2-2	**1**	**2**

SOSA	PACE	GRIFFEY
9	**81**	**18**

FINAL: Giants 9, Cardinals 6 (17 innings)

Cardinals' record: 25-23

397 ft.

This one landed on the loge reserved level in left field at Busch Stadium.

McGwire's impressive home run. "The ballpark is too small for him."

The homer was McGwire's 12th in 14 games and seventh in his last five, including four against the Giants. Finally convinced that it makes little sense to play with fire, San Francisco manager Dusty Baker ordered his pitcher to walk McGwire intentionally in the 14th inning—with two out and nobody on base. It was McGwire's third intentional pass of the game.

The Giants finally ended the 5-hour, 45-minute marathon when they scored three times in the 17th inning off lefthander Kent Mercker, the sixth Cardinals pitcher and a desperation choice out of a depleted St. Louis bullpen. Mercker had worked into the ninth inning of his previous start two days earlier.

RUTH *The two-homer performance against the last-place Boston Red Sox (Nos. 23 and 24) came off lefthander Hal Wiltse in the opener of a June 22 doubleheader and keyed a New York sweep.*

MARIS *An eighth-inning, two-run shot provided the icing for a 9-0 Yankees victory June 18 at Tiger Stadium. Maris' 24th homer, off righthander Jerry Casale, came in New York's 62nd game.*

■ "Walk McGwire with nobody on? That's a legend. People will be wondering if they did that with Babe Ruth." *—Giants pitcher Orel Hershiser*

■ "Your first instinct is like, no. Then you realize it's him and you say, 'Oh well, I guess so.' He's going pretty good right now." *—Giants pitcher Jim Poole, who walked McGwire intentionally in the 14th inning*

25

"(McGwire) only hit one today. Evidently Thomson was very good."

—Cardinals manager Tony La Russa, on the work of Rockies starter John Thomson

McGwire's first-inning home run did not have much meaning in the context of a 6-1 loss to Colorado, but it did add fuel to his rise as the pre-eminent power hitter in today's game.

"It's the greatest show on Earth," said Rockies left fielder Dante Bichette. "It's fun to watch him hit."

Big Mac's 433-foot blast off righthander John Thomson bounced off the window of Busch's Stadium Club, a restaurant tucked just below the upper deck. "He probably scared the people in there," quipped Rockies right fielder Larry Walker. "They probably

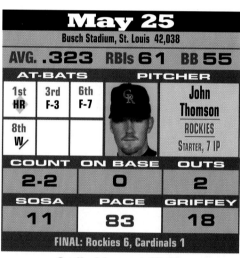

May 25
Busch Stadium, St. Louis 42,038

AVG. .323	RBIs 61	BB 55

AT-BATS			PITCHER	
1st HR	3rd F-3	6th F-7		John Thomson
8th W/				ROCKIES STARTER, 7 IP

COUNT	ON BASE	OUTS
2-2	0	2

SOSA	PACE	GRIFFEY
11	83	18

FINAL: Rockies 6, Cardinals 1

Cardinals' record: 25-24

This home run ball bounced off the Stadium Club below Big Mac Land in left field.

dropped their lobster."

With the homer, McGwire became the only player in major league history to reach 25 home runs before June 1. It was his fifth homer in four games, ninth in seven and 13th in 15. It also gave Big Mac 30 homers in 49 games at Busch Stadium and a career mark of one home run every 11.60 at-bats—keeping him ahead of Babe Ruth's 11.76 pace.

McGwire's homer was the only major mistake Thomson made while working seven five-hit innings. He had entered the game with a 2-5 record and 6.47 ERA, but after allowing Mac's first-inning homer he retired him on a popup and a line drive. McGwire's homer also extended the Cardinals' team-record streak of games with at least one home run, to 17. Big Mac hit 13 of the team's 34 during that stretch.

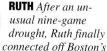

RUTH *After an unusual nine-game drought, Ruth finally connected off Boston's Slim Harriss. Babe's 25th homer, a two-run shot, was hit on June 30 at Yankee Stadium, in the team's 70th game.*

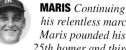

MARIS *Continuing his relentless march, Maris pounded his 25th homer and third in as many days, off A's lefty Jim Archer, in a June 19 game at Kansas City. It was the 63rd game for the Yankees.*

■ "Sometimes guys think about the third hitter (McGwire) and forget about the first two. He's going to get his home runs, and you're not going to prevent them." —*Rockies manager Don Baylor*

■ "I'm very comfortable mentally. There's nobody who's going to get into my mind." —*McGwire*

26

"I've got to get my thesaurus out and look for synonyms for incredible. You have to be awestruck by what he's done."

——Cardinals catcher Tom Lampkin

McGwire's bat continued to generate offensive headlines, but the big first baseman preferred to deflect attention toward a Cardinals pitcher after an impressive victory over San Diego.

"Petkovsek," McGwire said with a gesture toward the other side of the locker room, "had one hell of a game."

Big Mac was referring to righthander Mark Petkovsek, who shut out the Padres on four hits over eight innings while raising his record against them to 7-0. The Padres' runs were

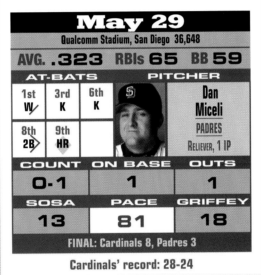

May 29

Qualcomm Stadium, San Diego 36,648

AVG. .323	RBIs 65	BB 59

AT-BATS			PITCHER
1st W/	3rd K	6th K	**Dan Miceli** PADRES Reliever, 1 IP
8th 2B	9th HR		

COUNT	ON BASE	OUTS
0-1	1	1

SOSA	PACE	GRIFFEY
13	81	18

FINAL: Cardinals 8, Padres 3

Cardinals' record: 28-24

McGwire's 26th homer sailed over the palm trees that line the left center field seats at Qualcomm Stadium.

scored in the ninth inning, two on Greg Vaughn's 17th homer.

"If they flashed a stat like that about someone else, you'd say, 'Man, he's got their number,'" Petkovsek said. "But when it comes to yourself. ..."

Petkovsek's shutout pitching was in danger of going for naught after seven innings because San Diego starter Joey Hamilton was strangling the Cardinals' offense as well. But then McGwire and company broke the game open.

McGwire keyed a six-run Cardinals eighth with a two-run, bases-loaded double. He then drove an 0-1, ninth-inning pitch from Dan Miceli over the fence in left-center, after Delino DeShields had reached on an error. It was Big Mac's first homer in three games but his 10th in an 11-game span. The four RBIs raised his major league-leading total to 65.

RUTH *Homer No. 26 was delivered off Senators righthander Hod Lisenbee in a July 3 game at Washington. Lisenbee would go on to finish his best career season with an 18-9 record.*

MARIS *After hitting a homer in his fourth consecutive game, Maris stood at 26 through 64 games. The first-inning solo shot came in a June 20 at-bat against Kansas City lefty Joe Nuxhall.*

■ "It's really unbelievable what he's done with all the pressures he has to endure every day." —*Cardinals manager Tony La Russa*

■ "What he's done is unbelievable, because he hardly knows the pitchers in this league." —*Cardinals coach Carney Lansford*

FLIGHT PATTERN: *Young St. Louisans Phillip Hunt (yellow shirt) and Ryan Klippel watch home run No. 25 hit the Stadium Club at Busch Stadium—a 433-footer on the Big Mac charts.*

27

"I didn't know how good I hit it until it was gone."

—McGwire

The McGwire home run parade continued when he drove a first-inning pitch from San Diego starter Andy Ashby 423 feet over the fence in left-center. As the accolades piled up, so did the incredible statistical asides.

The home run gave Big Mac 16 for the month of May, a Cardinals' single-month record. It gave him 11 homers in his last 11 games and 15 over a 19-game span. After shattering the major league record for

May 30
Qualcomm Stadium, San Diego 54,089

AVG. .324	RBIs 66	BB 60

AT-BATS			PITCHER	
1st HR	3rd W/	5th F-9		Andy Ashby
8th K				PADRES STARTER, 9 IP

COUNT	ON BASE	OUTS
0-1	0	2

SOSA	PACE	GRIFFEY
13	83	18

FINAL: Padres 3, Cardinals 2

Cardinals' record: 28-25

For the second straight game, Mac's left center field blast cleared the palm trees that line the outfield wall at Qualcomm Stadium.

most home runs by the end of May, McGwire needed only five more to claim the June mark. But most of the talk about McGwire's feats still focused on quality over quantity.

"A guy that strong and the way he's swinging the bat, I mean he got the best of it," said Ashby after surrendering McGwire's 16th 1998 homer of 400 feet or better. Ashby issued McGwire's 60th walk in the third, got him on a fly ball in the fifth and retired him on a called third strike as the leadoff batter in the eighth inning with the Cardinals leading 2-1.

"I wasn't going to lay one in there," Ashby said. "Lord willing, it worked out that way that one didn't come back across the plate. He got me once and I got him once."

In the end, the Padres got the Cardinals by scoring an unearned ninth-inning run.

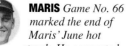

RUTH *Detroit right-hander Don Hankins served up Ruth's 27th home run in the nightcap of a July 8 double-header at Navin Field. The three-run shot propelled the Yankees to a 10-8 win.*

MARIS *Game No. 66 marked the end of Maris' June hot streak. He connected off Kansas City righthander Norm Bass in a June 22 game and brought to completion a run of nine homers in 12 games.*

■ "Any time a guy is that big, he kind of blocks out the sun. But any time you keep him in the ballpark the way he's swinging the bat, it's a moral victory." —*Padres pitcher Kevin Brown*

■ "He hits them out of sight. You can see mine." —*Cardinals outfielder Ron Gant*

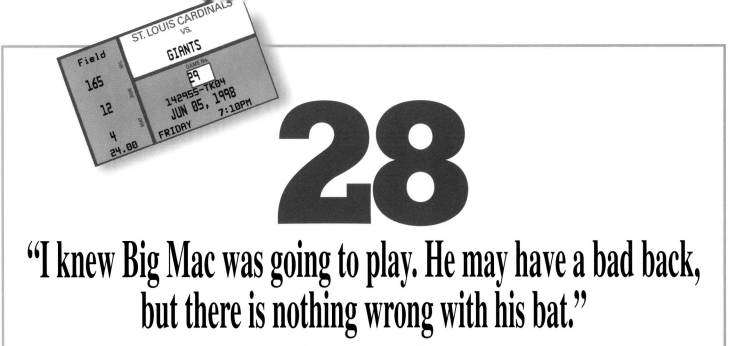

ST. LOUIS CARDINALS vs. GIANTS

Field 165 12 4
GAME No. 29
142955-TK04
JUN 05, 1998 7:10PM
FRIDAY
24.00

28

"I knew Big Mac was going to play. He may have a bad back, but there is nothing wrong with his bat."

—*Giants manager Dusty Baker*

It didn't take long for the McGwire express to regain top speed after three days of preventive maintenance. After sitting out three games to keep minor back spasms from becoming a long-term problem, Big Mac made an agile defensive play in the top of the first against San Francisco and then hit a 409-foot home run in the bottom of the inning.

The two-run shot over the center field fence off Orel Hershiser validated Cardinals manager Tony La Russa's decision to put McGwire in the lineup after watching him drill several tape-measure homers in batting practice. The homer was all the offense the Cardinals could muster en route to a third consecutive loss, which dropped them a game below .500.

"It's not like I planned on having a break," McGwire said after hitting his 18th Busch

June 5
Busch Stadium, St. Louis 43,239

AVG. .324	RBIs 70	BB 61

AT-BATS			PITCHER
1st HR	4th K	5th W	**Orel Hershiser**
7th 1B	9th K		GIANTS STARTER, 6 IP

COUNT	ON BASE	OUTS
1-2	1	1

SOSA	PACE	GRIFFEY
17	77	22

FINAL: Giants 3, Cardinals 2

Cardinals' record: 29-30

This home run landed in the first row of bleachers behind the Cardinals logo in left center field.

409 ft.

Stadium home run, a Cardinals season record at Busch. "But sometimes they're good for you."

McGwire felt a twinge in his back while grounding out during a game at San Diego and immediately put himself on the shelf. The development was reminiscent of back problems that have cost him major chunks of seasons past.

But he looked healthy enough against the Giants, also drawing his eighth intentional walk and smashing a drive off the left field wall that netted him only a single.

 RUTH *Homers 28 and 29 came in quick succession against righthander Ken Holloway in the opener of a July 9 doubleheader at Detroit. This was the fourth multihomer game of the season for Ruth.*

 MARIS *After seven homerless games, Maris resumed his march with a game-tying shot in the ninth inning of a July 1 game vs. Washington. Mickey Mantle followed with a game-ending homer.*

■ "I was a little too arrogant in thinking that I could get him out on that slider. I should have set him up better first." —*Giants pitcher Orel Hershiser*

■ "It's a mind game. If you say to yourself you're going to be slow, you're going to be slow. This game is mental and I was mentally prepared today." —*McGwire*

'A glimpse inside The Chase'

"Excuse me, Mark. I'm a writer. Can I have some of your time for a story I'm doing?"

It began tamely, though regularly. A steady parade that was maybe a nuisance at times, since so many of the reporters' questions got to be the same, about why he stayed in St. Louis instead of pursuing free agency, and whether anyone could break Roger Maris' record, and what he thought of as he ran the bases after a home run.

A nuisance like the incessant ring of the doorbell on Halloween. And then another ring. And another. But McGwire kept giving out the candy with a smile.

McGwire always had been a relatively shy man, and he couldn't understand what more there was to say about hitting home runs.

Understanding how miserable it had made Maris in 1961, he and the Cardinals decided it was best to organize the growing mob of reporters into a little party. The team would arrive in a new town and on the first day, McGwire would show up with a cup of coffee and lean against a wall in a hallway or the dugout or some out-of-the-way empty room at the stadium. Informally, he would answer many of the same questions he'd been answering since early March.

There would be five reporters, eight, a dozen. There soon would be 20, 25.

As the home runs piled up and the crush of bodies seemed to suffocate at times, the pressure to turn his daily job into an all-out pursuit of a record became more intense. Yet he knew he couldn't make it go away.

So he tried to laugh, joke, reveal a little of himself while protecting so much more. Reporters came looking for treats. He let them through the door, but they couldn't walk around and get anything more than what he dished out.

McGwire tried to keep his talks informal, even though he finally had to sit at a table in front of the 100 or so who wanted a glimpse inside The Chase.

And McGwire never seemed to run out of candy.

29

"They ought to charge people just to watch this."

—Utah Jazz basketball star Karl Malone, after watching McGwire's batting practice

As McGwire home runs kept sailing out of major league parks at a record pace, personal milestones provided little consolation for baseball's top gate attraction.

"We've been coming up short the last six games," he said after the Cardinals had lost their first 1998 interleague game, to the Chicago White Sox. "Nothing's clicking. It's not great and it's not fun. I don't care how you do individually, if you don't win as a team, it doesn't matter."

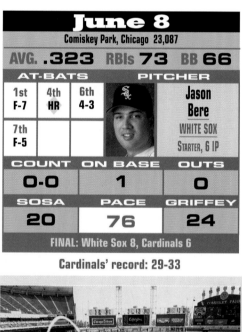

June 8
Comiskey Park, Chicago 23,087

AVG. .323	RBIs 73	BB 66

AT-BATS			PITCHER
1st F-7	4th HR	6th 4-3	Jason Bere
7th F-5			WHITE SOX STARTER, 6 IP

COUNT	ON BASE	OUTS
0-0	1	0

SOSA	PACE	GRIFFEY
20	76	24

FINAL: White Sox 8, Cardinals 6

Cardinals' record: 29-33

356 ft.

This towering fly ball barely cleared the wall and landed in the open area in front of Comiskey Park's left field seats.

In what had become a familiar 1998 routine, McGwire put on a batting-practice show, then homered in the game, but the Cardinals lost.

The defeat was their ninth in 10 games, dropping them to nine games behind the Chicago Cubs and Houston, co-leaders in the N.L. Central Division.

Big Mac's towering drive off Jason Bere in the fourth inning settled into the left field seats, a comparatively compact 356 feet from the plate. The two-run homer was his second shortest of the season.

It cut the Cardinals' deficit to 3-2, and they tied the game on a John Mabry homer an inning later before a five-run Chicago fifth broke it open. McGwire's home run was his eighth at new Comiskey Park and 12th overall against the White Sox in Chicago. It also brought his league-leading RBI total to 73.

RUTH *Babe's two-homer barrage against Ken Holloway fueled the Yankees' 19-run outburst in the opener of the team's July 9 doubleheader against the outmanned Detroit Tigers.*

MARIS *For the second straight day, Maris went 3-for-5 vs. Washington, and he spiced his July 2 effort with two home runs. The first, his 29th, came off Pete Burnside, a three-time victim in '61.*

■ "McGwire's probably the top home run threat in baseball. He must be seeing the ball very well." —*White Sox pitcher Jason Bere*

■ "He makes the place electric. Fans jump to their feet just to see him hit one. Players also, but not the opposing manager." —*White Sox manager Jerry Manuel*

30

"He hits the ball every day where you say, 'Wow, look at that one.' You never get tired of watching it, either."

—*Cardinals third baseman Gary Gaetti*

The routine was becoming disgustingly familiar, and McGwire wasn't in any mood to discuss home runs. The Cardinals blew a four-run, ninth-inning lead, lost to the Chicago White Sox in 11 innings, and then tried to come to grips with their seventh loss in eight games and 10th in 12.

"Absolutely meaningless," McGwire said, referring to his three-run, third-inning blast off White Sox rookie Jim Parque that helped the Cardinals storm to a 7-0 lead. "You take a two-, three-, four-run lead into the ninth inning, you have to win those games."

June 10
Comiskey Park, Chicago 16,151

AVG. .320	RBIs 76	BB 68

AT-BATS			PITCHER
1st K	3rd HR	5th W	**Jim Parque**
7th 4-3	9th K	11th W	WHITE SOX STARTER, 5 IP

COUNT	ON BASE	OUTS
1-0	2	1

SOSA	PACE	GRIFFEY
20	76	25

FINAL: White Sox 10, Cardinals 8 (11 innings)

Cardinals' record: 30-34

The ball sailed just a few feet over the center field fence at Comiskey Park, landing in the open area behind the outfield wall.

With the help of McGwire's 409-foot drive into the center field backdrop at Comiskey Park, the Cardinals carried an 8-4 lead into the ninth. But Chicago's Albert Belle hit his second three-run homer of the game and Robin Ventura followed with a bases-empty shot that forced extra innings. Ventura's second homer, a two-run blast in the 11th, gave Chicago an unlikely victory.

McGwire's 18th homer in a 27-game span allowed him to reach the 30 plateau for the ninth time. It was the result of curious strategy by Chicago manager Jerry Manuel, who refused to take the normal course by walking Big Mac with runners on second and third and one out. The three RBIs lifted McGwire's N.L.-leading total to 76 and kept him on pace to top Hack Wilson's single-season record of 190.

RUTH *Halfway home. Cleveland lefty Joe Shaute became Ruth's 20th different victim, and the Yankees rolled past the Indians, 7-0. Home run No. 30 came in the team's 83rd game on July 12.*

MARIS *The third multihomer game of Maris' season was punctuated by a two-run, seventh-inning blast off Washington's Johnny Klippstein. On July 2, after 75 games, he was halfway to 60.*

■ "I can remember over in the American League when they were saying if there was something up, he can't catch up with it. And you could pitch him there. But not any longer. You pitch McGwire up and you're going to allow more home runs than if you pitch him down." —*Cardinals manager Tony La Russa*

31

"He's a part of the game we should be proud of. There's something there people want to see."

—Diamondbacks manager Buck Showalter

McGwire reached the halfway point of his record-breaking home run quest the same way he started it—with a grand slam that keyed a Cardinals' victory. But until he had crossed the plate and performed his arm-bumping ritual with celebrating team-mates, he didn't even realize what he had done.

"I don't want to be ignorant, but I didn't know it was a grand slam," McGwire said after helping the Cardinals post only their second win in nine games. "I was into trying to really mentally prepare myself against Andy (Benes) because he got me out the first time, so I wasn't aware of who was on base—and I guess maybe it helped me out."

McGwire's 438-foot blow into the seats in left-center at Arizona's Bank One Ballpark came off former teammate

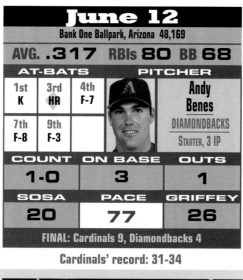

June 12
Bank One Ballpark, Arizona 48,169

AVG. .317	RBIs 80	BB 68

AT-BATS			PITCHER
1st K	3rd HR	4th F-7	**Andy Benes**
7th F-8	9th F-3		DIAMONDBACKS STARTER, 3 IP

COUNT	ON BASE	OUTS
1-0	3	1

SOSA	PACE	GRIFFEY
20	77	26

FINAL: Cardinals 9, Diamondbacks 4

Cardinals' record: 31-34

McGwire hit his 31st homer deep into the seats in left center at Bank One Ballpark.

Benes, who had struck him out in the first inning. Benes, who was projected as the ace of the Cardinals' 1998 staff, chose instead to sign a big free-agent contract with the Diamond-backs in February.

The homer keyed an eight-run, third-inning uprising that also included a three-run homer by shortstop Royce Clayton, who scored two runs in the in-ning. McGwire's 11th career grand slam also was his 15th home run in 20 games.

Not only did the 48,169 fans get to see a memorable home run, many were present for a batting-practice wallop that landed on a ledge above the American flag in left-center field and bounced through a window onto Jefferson Street—the first ball to be hit out of the new park. The ledge is 483 feet from home plate and 89 feet above the field.

RUTH *White Sox righthander Tommy Thomas became a two-time victim when he served up Ruth's 31st home run, a third-inning solo shot, in a July 24 game at Chicago's Comiskey Park.*

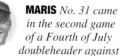
MARIS *No. 31 came in the second game of a Fourth of July doubleheader against Detroit at Yankee Stadium. The victim was righthander Frank Lary, who would go on to post a 23-9 record in 1961.*

■ "The fans got to see what they wanted to see. I didn't see what I wanted to see. Maybe it took their attention away from a bad outing for me. It's just bad pitches and bad results." *—Diamondbacks pitcher Andy Benes*

■ "It's overwhelming. I've never seen it. I don't think any other baseball player has seen it." *—McGwire, on the intense fan interest engulfing him*

FLIGHT OF PHOENIX:
Big Mac's first visit to Bank One Ballpark attracted the usual expectant fans and featured his second grand slam of the season—this one off former teammate Andy Benes.

This Is Houston's Brand of Baseball!

32

"They're showing batting practice on TV. ... They were broadcasting it play-by-play in Phoenix. Now that's psycho."

—McGwire

On a night in which they registered one of their most dramatic wins of the season, the Houston Astros felt the full impact of the McGwire phenomenon.

Many of the 37,147 fans who earlier had witnessed McGwire's major league-leading 32nd homer departed after his ninth-inning at-bat and didn't see the Astros rally with four ninth-inning runs.

"I understand that a lot of people come out to see Mark McGwire, but they should be out here to see the Houston Astros play the St. Louis Cardinals," said Astros first baseman Jeff Bagwell, who contributed a two-run homer to the winning rally. "For them to leave after Mark's last at-bat, I wouldn't say it was a slap in the face, but unfortunately for them, they missed a good inning."

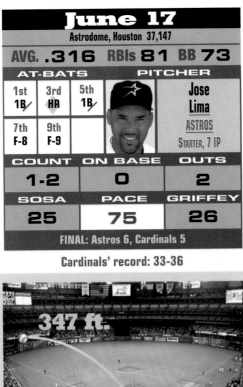

June 17
Astrodome, Houston 37,147

AVG. **.316** RBIs **81** BB **73**

AT-BATS			PITCHER
1st 1B	3rd HR	5th 1B	Jose Lima
7th F-8	9th F-9		ASTROS STARTER, 7 IP

COUNT	ON BASE	OUTS
1-2	0	2

SOSA	PACE	GRIFFEY
25	75	26

FINAL: Astros 6, Cardinals 5

Cardinals' record: 33-36

347 ft.

A low line drive cleared the top left corner of the Astrodome scoreboard in left field.

McGwire had helped the Cardinals build a 5-2 lead with a third-inning drive over the scoreboard in left. The 347-footer off righthander Jose Lima, which equaled McGwire's shortest of the season, broke a 12-at-bat homerless streak and was his first at the Astrodome.

But it wasn't enough to save the Cardinals, who slid further behind the division-leading Astros. Houston rallied against Jeff Brantley and Curtis King. "You can't describe what it feels like to lose this game," Cardinals manager Tony La Russa said.

RUTH *The first of two July 26 home runs off righthander Milt Gaston came in the opener of a doubleheader against the St. Louis Browns at Yankee Stadium. It was Ruth's 11th first-inning homer.*

MARIS *Maris hit his 32nd home run in a July 5 game against Cleveland, the 78th game of the season for the Yankees. Frank Funk, a righthander, served up the seventh-inning blast.*

■ "If I hit a home run and we don't win, it doesn't matter. When you have a chance to be in two games and climb the ladder, especially against a team like Houston, it's really tough to lose one like this." —*McGwire*

■ "He's putting fans in the stands. They come to see him hit. Our job is to win and strike him out. He can keep putting fans in the seats and we can keep winning." —*Astros outfielder Carl Everett*

33

"He's the same as Aaron, Ruth or Williams. You've got to throw good stuff on the corners. Anything else is unacceptable."

—Astros manager Larry Dierker

McGwire didn't want to discuss long home runs, but the one he hit into the fifth deck of the Astrodome had longtime Houston baseball watchers scratching their heads. The left field solo shot was measured at 449 feet, but most observers thought that figure was conservative.

"This was three outstanding games for us," said McGwire, deflecting talk toward the Cardinals' win, which gave them two of three vs. the Astros. "This is what baseball is all about. I just want to play baseball. I play this game for one reason—to win."

After relenting on his

June 18		
Astrodome, Houston 43,806		
AVG. .317	RBIs 82	BB 75

AT-BATS			PITCHER	
1st 5-3	3rd W/	5th HR		Shane Reynolds
7th W/	9th F-9			ASTROS STARTER, 4⅓ IP

COUNT	ON BASE	OUTS
1-1	0	0

SOSA	PACE	GRIFFEY
25	76	27

FINAL: Cardinals 7, Astros 6

Cardinals' record: 34-36

449 ft.

This mammoth drive sailed into the left field upper deck at the Astrodome.

previous day's threat to stop taking batting practice because of the circus it had become, McGwire deposited 14 practice balls into the Astrodome seats, including four in the upper deck. He then ripped what might have been the longest home run in the history of the stadium. The fifth-inning shot, combined with home runs by Ron Gant and Ray Lankford, helped the Cardinals build a lead they never relinquished.

McGwire received a standing ovation from 43,806 fans as he rounded the bases. The homer was his sixth of the month and gave him the distinction of hitting more home runs than any player in history before the end of June.

That his homer apparently was mismeasured was the least of Big Mac's worries. "So be it," he said. "You don't win a prize for it."

 RUTH *After 95 games, Ruth stood at 33, thanks to his July 26 explosion against the Browns in the opener of a doubleheader. Milt Gaston became the fourth pitcher to serve up two homers in a game to him.*

 MARIS *After three quiet games, Maris resumed his quest with a seventh-inning homer off Bill Monbouquette in the opening game of a July 9 doubleheader against Boston at Yankee Stadium.*

■ "It (the June home run record) is a great honor, but I can't sit back and think about it. You've got to think about tomorrow. You don't have time to think about what you've done." *—McGwire*

Some days are better than others

McGwire's road to baseball's home run record was not traveled without some bumps and unexpected turns.

There were stretches when the remarkable consistency he exhibited through most of the season gave way to the angst suffered by any man on a mission.

After opening the season with four home runs in four games, the Cardinals first baseman struggled through an eight-game drought that ended with a three-homer purge against the Arizona Diamondbacks.

There were other slow times, but not many. One was a five-game homerless stretch between his June 18 homer at Houston and the 433-foot shot he hit at Cleveland off Jaret Wright June 24. And there was the early August slump that allowed Sammy Sosa to pull back into the home run chase.

But the frustration, the hard looks and the angst always ended with another home run barrage.

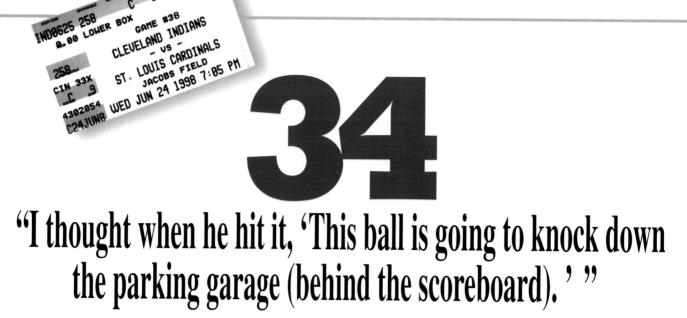

34

"I thought when he hit it, 'This ball is going to knock down the parking garage (behind the scoreboard).'"

—Indians manager Mike Hargrove

Five games and 18 at-bats after hitting home run No. 33, McGwire ended one of the longest droughts of his season with a 433-foot drive off Cleveland starter Jaret Wright. The ball fell just short of the massive Jacobs Field scoreboard in left field, but it looked short and unimportant on the scoreboard.

"It's really insignificant," McGwire said, after watching the Indians score seven runs in a marathon first inning en route to a lopsided victory. "We got a good butt-whipping today."

McGwire connected with the bases empty in the fourth inning, cutting the Cardinals' deficit to 7-1. The majestic fly ball settled just short of the scoreboard that only McGwire had reached during a regular-season game. He received a standing ovation from the sellout crowd of 43,321 as he circled the bases. Big Mac was removed

June 24
Jacobs Field, Cleveland 43,321

AVG. .316	RBIs 83	BB 78

AT-BATS			PITCHER
1st 1B/	4th HR	6th F-4	Jaret Wright
			INDIANS
			STARTER, 6⅓ IP

COUNT	ON BASE	OUTS
1-1	0	1

SOSA	PACE	GRIFFEY
31	72	30

FINAL: Indians 14, Cardinals 3

Cardinals' record: 38-38

This home run landed near the top of the left field bleachers, just below the Jacobs Field scoreboard.

from the game in the sixth inning of a 12-2 blowout and, ironically, Brian Hunter, his replacement, stepped to the plate with the bases loaded in the seventh.

"So if McGwire hits a grand slam it's 12-7. So what?" Cardinals manager Tony La Russa told inquiring reporters. "We've been talking about needing to give Mark a day off between now and Monday, when we're off. What this means is, he can play now."

The homer was McGwire's 29th against the Indians, including 19 in Cleveland and eight at Jacobs Field. It brought back memories of the 485-foot rocket he hit off righthander Orel Hershiser in a 1997 game. That homer, which dented a beer advertisement on the scoreboard, was the longest in Jacobs Field history.

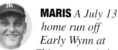
■ "They're an outstanding team. When you give them a seven-run first inning, your backs are really against the wall." —McGwire

■ "If there's one guy in baseball who we want to do it, it's him. It's truly a pleasure to watch him, to watch how he handles himself. He's such a gentleman." —Indians first baseman Jim Thome

35

"I feel sorry for Burba. But I enjoyed this one as much as Hershiser's. It's amazing to see a ball travel that far."

—Indians shortstop Omar Vizquel

Cardinals fans trying to find a bright side to two one-sided losses in Cleveland needed look no further than the massive Jacobs Field scoreboard—more specifically, a steel support crossbeam connected to the structure.

"It makes your stomach feel funny when he hits them," said Indians manager Mike Hargrove, referring to the first-inning, 461-foot McGwire blast that struck the beam and bounced back onto the field, eluding the grasp of straining fans. "They just go so far and so high. I'd pay to watch him hit."

The homer, which gave the Cardinals a temporary 1-0 lead, was the second-longest ever hit at The Jake—24 feet shorter than the acclaimed 485-foot drive McGwire bounced off the scoreboard vs. Orel Hershiser in 1997. Only the beam, positioned between the left field foul pole and the scoreboard,

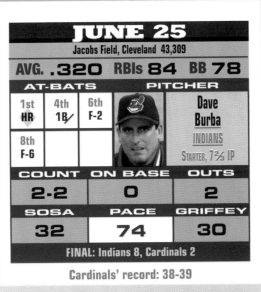

JUNE 25

Jacobs Field, Cleveland 43,309

AVG. **.320** RBIs **84** BB **78**

AT-BATS			PITCHER
1st **HR**	4th **1B/**	6th **F-2**	**Dave Burba**
8th **F-6**			INDIANS STARTER, 7⅔ IP

COUNT	ON BASE	OUTS
2-2	0	2

SOSA	PACE	GRIFFEY
32	74	30

FINAL: Indians 8, Cardinals 2

Cardinals' record: 38-39

McGwire's towering blast hit the crossbeam that supports the Jacobs Field scoreboard in left field.

kept it from leaving the 5-year-old ballpark. It was McGwire's ninth homer at The Jake, more than any other visiting player.

"I thought it was foul," said Indians righthander Dave Burba. "I looked in for a new ball and Sandy (Alomar) was just staring. I never saw the ball. Apparently, it went pretty far."

McGwire was typically unimpressed by his latest strongman feat. "I just don't like losing," he said. "I'm sort of disappointed in the way it went here."

The two-game series was viewed by 86,630 Cleveland fans who were exposed to the best of both worlds—two long McGwire home runs as well as two routs by the Indians.

RUTH *A struggling Ruth finally broke his seven-game homer drought with an August 5 smash off Detroit righthander George Smith. With 35 homers in 106 games, Ruth needed to pick up his pace.*

MARIS *Unlike Ruth, Maris was moving in the fast lane through only 86 games. His 35th, a solo shot in a July 15 contest at Chicago, came in the third inning against righthander Ray Herbert.*

■ "(McGwire) is like the Empire State Building standing there with a bat in his hands. Words can't describe how good he is—to keep doing it day after day with the media pressure. I would have liked to see Ruth and him in the same era." *—Indians first baseman Jim Thome, who hit two home runs in the game*

■ "It's just not good losing. I don't think anybody enjoys it. We get on a roll, and then we come up to a brick wall. It's just not fun." *—McGwire*

36

"He's not just a power hitter, he's a great hitter. I had him 0-2 and he battled. He made it happen."

—Twins pitcher Mike Trombley

The McGwire home run and batting practice parade, weaving its way through major league ballparks throughout the country, was getting rave reviews as he maintained his record pace approaching the All-Star break. And Big Mac seemed a bit stunned by the emotional reaction of crowds in opposing ballparks.

"This has never happened to me and I don't know if it's happened to anybody else," he said after his 36th homer, at the

June 27
Metrodome, Minnesota 35,002

AVG. .313	RBIs 86	BB 79

AT-BATS			PITCHER
1st K	4th F-7	6th W√	**Mike Trombley**
7th HR	9th F-8		TWINS
			Reliever, 1⅔ IP

COUNT	ON BASE	OUTS
2-2	1	2

SOSA	PACE	GRIFFEY
32	74	31

FINAL: Cardinals 7, Twins 2

Cardinals' record: 39-40

Fans in the left center field seats at the Metrodome swarmed to catch McGwire's 36th home run ball.

Minneapolis Metrodome, was greeted by a roar that grew to a crescendo from 35,002 pumped-up Twins fans. "But it's a great feeling and I wish every ballplayer could feel the way I feel."

McGwire's seventh-inning blast, a towering 431-foot, two-run shot to left-center, extended a 4-1 Cardinals' lead and helped gain a much-needed victory. It was Big Mac's 60th home run in 124 games with the Cardinals and only his second hit in 10 career at-bats vs. the Twins' Mike Trombley.

The Cardinals ended a four-game losing streak and won for the first time ever at the Metrodome—site of their seventh-game World Series loss to the Twins in 1987. McGwire's 36th home run tied him for most by a Cardinals player since Hall of Famer Stan Musial hit that many in 1949.

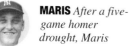

RUTH *Snapping a three-game hitless skid, Ruth pounded his 36th homer, a three-run, third-inning shot off Senators lefty Tom Zachary in an August 10 game at Washington's Griffith Stadium.*

MARIS *After a five-game homer drought, Maris returned to form with a solo blast in a July 21 game at Boston. For the second time in two weeks, righthander Bill Monbouquette was the victim.*

■ "It amazes me. It's overwhelming. It's almost like I'm sort of speechless. What do you say? Basically, thank you." —*McGwire, on the reaction he was getting from opposing fans*

■ "The best thing going now in baseball is Mark McGwire. Baseball needs it. I think it's a great thing. The fans ought to be applauded for recognizing that he's got a chance to do something special every time he steps to the plate." —*Cardinals pitcher Todd Stottlemyre*

37

"It's pretty awesome.
I'm sure we'll read all about it tomorrow."

—Cardinals third baseman Gary Gaetti

Kansas City lefthander Glendon Rusch shudders at the thought of giving up home runs, but he had to appreciate the one McGwire hit into the upper deck at Busch Stadium in an otherwise forgettable Cardinals loss. The blast was so majestic that the fireworks signaling a Cardinals' home run ignited even before the ball settled into the crowd.

"It was impressive," said Rusch, who had shut out the Cardinals for six innings before McGwire gave one of his fastballs a 472-foot ride. "I turned around and watched, just

June 30
Busch Stadium, St. Louis 41,801

AVG. **.319**	RBIs **87**	BB **79**

AT-BATS			PITCHER
1st 2B▷	4th 1B/	7th HR	**Glendon Rusch**
9th 5-3			ROYALS STARTER, 7⅔ IP

COUNT	ON BASE	OUTS
0-1	0	0

SOSA	PACE	GRIFFEY
33	74	33

FINAL: Royals 6, Cardinals 1

Cardinals' record: 39-42

This upper-deck home run landed on the Busch Stadium walkway behind and to the right of Big Mac Land.

472 ft.

like everybody else did."

The blast tied Reggie Jackson's record for home runs before the All-Star break—but in a lot fewer games. Jackson had 37 in 92 games for Oakland in 1969; McGwire's 37th came in the 81st game—with five games remaining before the midsummer classic. Jackson went on to hit only 10 more the rest of the season.

True to form, McGwire chose to focus on the Cardinals' sixth loss in seven games and dismal 3-8 interleague record, the worst in baseball. "You just hope that something clicks," he said. "Sometimes you think, 'What is it?' and then all of a sudden the next thing you know, you're on a 10-game winning streak. Anything can happen at any given time."

The homer was McGwire's 32nd in 60 career games at Busch Stadium.

RUTH *The Babe connected for a third time off White Sox righthander Tommy Thomas in an August 16 game at Chicago's Comiskey Park. The bases-empty homer ended a three-game homerless streak.*

MARIS *The biggest day of Maris' season began with a fourth-inning homer off Chicago lefty Frank Baumann in the opener of a July 25 doubleheader. He would hit three more before the day was over.*

■ "It says a lot when a guy's pitching a shutout against you and that's the only run you get. He's done it a lot of times against really good pitching. The pitch that he hit was no mistake—a fastball kind of up and on the inner part of the plate. That ties up a lot of hitters, but he hits it 400 feet." *—Cardinals manager Tony La Russa*

■ "McGwire is so focused and locked in right now, it's unbelievable. He may disagree, but I see him hit a ball out of the ballpark on *SportsCenter* every night." *—Royals manager Tony Muser*

McGwire shorts out in the All-Star homer contest

Everybody came to see Mark McGwire, but what they got was Ken Griffey Jr. That's not a bad consolation prize.

The event was baseball's annual home run-hitting contest, and the thought of McGwire lining up pitches in the rarefied air of home run-friendly Coors Field was enough to make expectant fans drool with delight. But as McGwire and his batting practice pitcher struggled to get in sync, other All-Stars took center stage.

Big Mac managed only four home runs on 14 swings and delivered only one of his trademark moonshots. But Griffey, a last-minute contest entry, hit several upper-deck drives en route to eventual victory.

McGwire was hitless in two at-bats in the All-Star Game the next day.

38

"I feel all right. I've just been a millimeter off. There hasn't been a guy alive who's been on all year. I'm human."

—McGwire

With the Houston Astros hovering above the pack in the National League Central Division, it was a bit easier for them to appreciate some good, old-fashioned drama at their expense.

"I don't like losing, but for a Cardinal fan, it doesn't get any more exciting than that," said first baseman Jeff Bagwell. "Extra innings. Team down by a run, man on base. Mark McGwire coming up against a guy throwing 98 miles per hour. That's classic."

So was the 485-foot bomb that exploded off his bat and landed above the Big Mac Land section of seats just inside the left field foul pole in Busch Stadium's upper deck. The distance seemed conservative, prompting Astros closer Billy Wagner, Mac's latest victim, to roll his eyes and suggest, "Somebody up

July 11
Busch Stadium, St. Louis 45,760

AVG. .306	RBIs 89	BB 91

AT-BATS			PITCHER
1st K	4th F-3	6th 1-3	**Billy Wagner**
9th W/	11th HR		ASTROS RELIEVER, ⅓ IP

COUNT	ON BASE	OUTS
0-2	1	1

SOSA	PACE	GRIFFEY
35	69	37

FINAL: Cardinals 4, Astros 3 (11 innings)

Cardinals' record: 42-47

485 ft.

This game-winning homer sailed into Busch's left field upper deck near Big Mac Land.

there can't count."

McGwire's first home run in eight games came in the bottom of the 11th inning, after the Astros had taken a 3-2 lead on Bill Spiers' bases-loaded sacrifice fly. McGwire pounded an 0-2 Wagner fastball clocked at 97 mph, sending the packed house of 45,760 into a wild celebration.

"Right at contact, I knew it was gone. It was the easiest swing I had all day," said McGwire, who had gone 21 at-bats without a homer, his second-longest drought of the season. In that stretch, Big Mac was walked 12 times and hit by a pitch.

Before ending Wagner's streak of 19 consecutive successful save chances, Big Mac had struck out, fouled out, grounded out and walked—his major league-leading 91st base on balls of the season.

RUTH *The Babe made No. 38 a dramatic one, connecting off Chicago righthander Sarge Connally in the 11th inning of an August 17 game at Comiskey Park. The homer gave New York a 3-2 win.*

MARIS *His second home run in the opener of the July 25 doubleheader was hit off former Yankee World Series hero Don Larsen, now with the White Sox. No. 38 was hit in the team's 95th game.*

■ "He hit the tar out of that ball. I looked up and I couldn't find it. I thought it was out of the stadium." *—Astros closer Billy Wagner*

■ "He had gone 20 or so at-bats without hitting one, so you knew he was about to explode on somebody. I was hoping we could sneak out of here before it happened." *—Astros first baseman Jeff Bagwell*

39/40

"You've got to get that family of four out of the left field seats before he kills somebody."

—Astros second baseman Craig Biggio

Rejuvenated by his dramatic July 11 homer that beat Central Division-leading Houston, McGwire pounded two more in a series-ending victory over the Astros and became only the third player to reach the 40 plateau in the long history of the Cardinals franchise.

Big Mac connected for solo blasts off Sean Bergman, in the first inning, and rookie Scott Elarton, in the seventh. Both homers were 400-footers that easily cleared the left field wall. In reaching the 40-homer plateau for the fifth time, McGwire joined Rogers Hornsby (42 in 1922) and Johnny Mize (43 in 1940) as the only Cardinals to reach that figure. Stan Musial, the franchise's career home run leader, could do no better than 39 in 1948. No one in baseball history had reached the 40 mark in fewer at-bats

July 12
Busch Stadium, St. Louis 45,485

AVG. .310	RBIs 91	BB 92

AT-BATS			PITCHER
1st HR	3rd K	4th W/	**Sean Bergman** STARTER, 5 IP
7th HR			**Scott Elarton** RELIEVER, 2 IP

COUNT	ON BASE	OUTS
0-0, 2-1	0,0	2,0

SOSA	PACE	GRIFFEY
35	72	37

FINAL: Cardinals 6, Astros 4

Cardinals' record: 43-47

405 ft.
415 ft.

The first homer was a line drive off the back wall of the visitors' bullpen in left field; the second landed in the seats behind the bullpen wall.

(281) than McGwire.

"To have my name pass those is remarkable," McGwire said. "For somebody who never thought he would play in the National League. ... I'm very proud to be with those guys and surpass them."

McGwire attributed his surge to 10-year-old son Matt, an occasional Cardinals batboy who gave his dad a special good-luck present before leaving St. Louis for his home in Southern California prior to the game. "He kissed my bat," a smiling McGwire told reporters. "The last time he kissed it, I hit three home runs."

McGwire, who moved past Hall of Famer Billy Williams into 23rd place on the career home run list with 427, also was issued his major league-leading 19th intentional walk and 92nd overall.

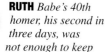

RUTH *Babe's 40th homer, his second in three days, was not enough to keep the Yankees from dropping their fourth straight game to the Indians, a 9-4 loss on August 22 at Cleveland.*

MARIS *Chicago's Russ Kemmerer and Warren Hacker served up 39 and 40 in the nightcap of a July 25 twin bill, completing Maris' four-home run day. His homers accounted for seven runs.*

■ "Sixty-four (homers) in 135 games (as a Cardinal). He's a pretty good pickup." *—Cardinals manager Tony La Russa*

■ "I've not been around too long, but the home run he hit off me was the most impressive thing I've seen in my major league career." *—Astros pitcher Scott Elarton*

■ "The first two games he didn't swing the bat very well. He's swinging pretty good now." *—Astros manager Larry Dierker*

GOING, GOING, GONE: *McGwire connects with a Sean Bergman pitch, the first of two home runs he would hit in a July 12 game against the Houston Astros at Busch Stadium.*

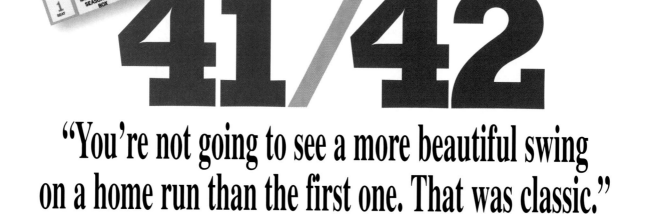

41/42

"You're not going to see a more beautiful swing on a home run than the first one. That was classic."

—Cardinals manager Tony La Russa

Two strikes, two more home runs. McGwire was the picture of efficiency as he keyed a Cardinals' victory over the Los Angeles Dodgers and kept his express rolling toward baseball's single-season home run record.

McGwire jumped on the first pitch from Brian Bohanon in the opening inning and connected with a 1-0 Antonio Osuna pitch in the eighth—the only strikes he would see during a game in which he drew his 98th and 99th walks. "I swung the bat twice tonight," McGwire said, "and I hit two home runs."

The first was a massive shot to left center that landed midway in the upper deck and was measured at 511 feet. The fourth-longest homer in Busch Stadium history (McGwire also hit the other three) was his fourth off Bohanon in nine

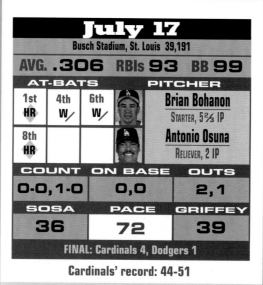

July 17
Busch Stadium, St. Louis 39,191

AVG. **.306**	RBIs **93**	BB **99**

AT-BATS			PITCHER
1st HR	4th W/	6th W/	**Brian Bohanon** STARTER, 5⅔ IP
8th HR			**Antonio Osuna** RELIEVER, 2 IP

COUNT	ON BASE	OUTS
0-0, 1-0	0,0	2,1

SOSA	PACE	GRIFFEY
36	72	39

FINAL: Cardinals 4, Dodgers 1

Cardinals' record: 44-51

The first home run hit the upper-deck walkway in left center; the second landed in the left field seats below the Stadium Club.

big-league at-bats.

"It was early in the game and I wanted to challenge him," Bohanon said. "I made a bad pitch and he hit it out. ... We've got a history together. He's a guy I've struggled against."

So Bohanon took measures to make sure it wouldn't happen again.

"He got me in the first at-bat, and in the second at-bat I decided I wasn't going to let him hit," he said. "I decided to take my chances with (Brian) Jordan. I hate doing that, but I felt like it was the best situation."

McGwire's eighth-inning shot, which traveled 425 feet to left, completed his fifth multi-homer effort of the season and the 48th of his career. It also tied him with Hall of Famer Rogers Hornsby for most home runs in a season by a righthanded-hitting Cardinal.

RUTH *No. 42 was served up by lefty Ernie Wingard in an August 28 game at St. Louis. Wingard would go on to finish the season at 2-13, the worst record of any of Ruth's 1927 victims.*

MARIS *After hitting his 42nd home run in an August 11 game at Washington, Maris still trailed Yankees teammate Mickey Mantle (44) in the American League home run race.*

■ "I don't diagnose things like that. You see it and you swing. I'm not a player that sits around and diagnoses a swing." —McGwire

■ "He hits my fastball, he hits my changeup, he hits my curveball. ... With the power he has, Yellowstone ain't going to hold him." —Dodgers pitcher Brian Bohanon

DEEP, DEEP THOUGHTS: By mid-July, McGwire was marching relentlessly toward his date with destiny. This two-home run performance against the Los Angeles Dodgers included a 511-foot bomb off shellshocked lefthander Brian Bohanon (above left).

43

"McGwire is probably the strongest power hitter of all time."

—Padres manager Bruce Bochy

Something about San Diego seems to bring out the best in McGwire, who grew up in the Los Angeles area and played collegiate baseball at USC. "Southern California. It's like coming home," he said after collecting four hits and his major league-leading 43rd home run in a romp past the Padres.

With son Matt watching from the dugout, Big Mac hit a two-run shot off Brian Boehringer that landed in Qualcomm Stadium's second deck, 458 feet from home plate in left-center field. The four-hit night lifted his 1998 average against the Padres to .429, with

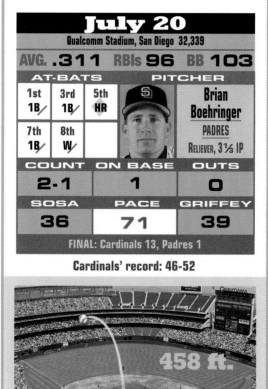

July 20

Qualcomm Stadium, San Diego 32,339

AVG. .311	RBIs 96	BB 103

AT-BATS / **PITCHER**

1st 1B	3rd 1B	5th HR
7th 1B	8th W	

Brian Boehringer
PADRES
Reliever, 3⅓ IP

COUNT	ON BASE	OUTS
2-1	1	0

SOSA	PACE	GRIFFEY
36	71	39

FINAL: Cardinals 13, Padres 1

Cardinals' record: 46-52

The ball sailed into the left center field seats of Qualcomm Stadium's second deck.

five homers and 15 RBIs in eight games. Three of the homers came in San Diego.

"We've matched up with them pretty well through all the games we've played," McGwire said after the Cardinals had snapped San Diego's five-game winning streak. "We haven't won all of them, but we've been in every game."

The homer allowed Big Mac to tie Johnny Mize's single-season record for homers by a Cardinal. Mize hit 43 in 1940. Ray Lankford added a grand slam and Royce Clayton homered and tripled, giving the top three batters in the lineup nine hits, with three homers, nine RBIs and seven runs scored. McGwire's home run opened up some breathing room between him and fellow record-chasers Ken Griffey (39) and Sammy Sosa (36).

RUTH *On the last day of August, Ruth connected off Boston righthander Tony Welzer. With 43 home runs in 127 Yankee games, the Bambino would need a big September finish.*

MARIS *Washington's Dick Donovan, who would finish as the A.L.'s ERA leader in 1961, joined Maris' hit list on August 12. Homer No. 43 pulled him to one behind A.L. leader Mickey Mantle.*

■ "There's no doubt he's a guy you can't make any mistakes against." —*Padres pitcher Mark Langston*

■ "I was sitting on the pitch and got hold of it. When you anticipate and get a good swing on it, you can drive it a long way." —*McGwire*

44

"The home run he hit was a slider. ... He's hit a lot of home runs. That's just his game."

—Rockies pitcher John Thomson

After he had seriously considered taking the day off, McGwire wrote a new page in the Cardinals' record book with a gargantuan 452-foot blast that gave 48,288 expectant fans at Colorado's Coors Field exactly what they had come to see.

Big Mac, who was struggling through an 0-for-16 slump that included the first two games of the Rockies series, drove a fourth-inning pitch from Colorado righthander John Thomson over the left field bleachers. The homer moved him past Hall of Famer Johnny Mize as the most prolific single-season slugger in the Cardinals' long history. Mize

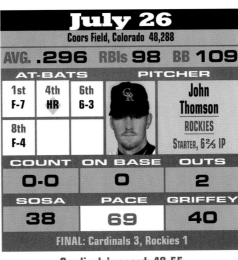

July 26
Coors Field, Colorado 48,288

AVG. .296	RBIs 98	BB 109

AT-BATS			PITCHER
1st F-7	4th HR	6th 6-3	**John Thomson** ROCKIES
8th F-4			STARTER, 6⅔ IP

COUNT	ON BASE	OUTS
0-0	0	2

SOSA	PACE	GRIFFEY
38	69	40

FINAL: Cardinals 3, Rockies 1

Cardinals' record: 49-55

452 ft.

McGwire's 44th home run, which cleared the left field bleachers at Coors Field, was caught by a fan in front of the concession stand.

posted his team-record 43 home runs in 1940.

"I would have loved to have had the day off today. But look what happened. I ran into one," said McGwire, who had played 18 straight games since the All-Star break. "I was dead. I should have had an off day sometime during this road trip, but we didn't do it. Sometimes a day off goes a long way. ..."

Johnny Mize

Thomson had retired 11 straight Cardinals when McGwire broke a scoreless tie, jump-starting a St. Louis victory.

It was his only hit of the night and his first home run at long ball-friendly Coors Field in six 1998 games. He had hit four in four games there after his 1997 trade to the Cardinals.

RUTH *Philadelphia lefty Rube Walberg, bringing out the best in Ruth for the fourth time, served up home run No. 44 as the September assault began during a 12-2 Yankees' victory.*

MARIS *Another multihomer day. His 44th came in the opener of an August 13 doubleheader at Washington and added righthander Bennie Daniels to Maris' ever-growing hit list.*

■ "I'm just learning the history of the Cardinals. I was stuck on the West Coast for 11 years and didn't really know much about the history of the Cardinals, but now I do and I'm happy to be a part of it." —*McGwire, after setting the team single-season home run record*

■ "You'd better go talk to those pitchers over there who don't throw me many strikes. You guys think they put it on a tee for me, and they don't." —*McGwire, explaining his recent slump*

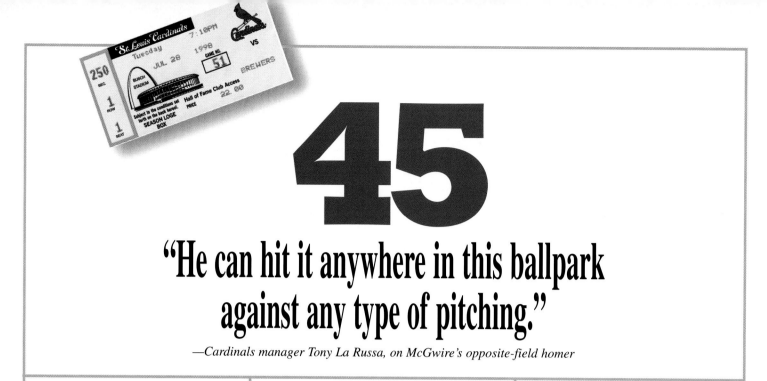

45

"He can hit it anywhere in this ballpark against any type of pitching."

—Cardinals manager Tony La Russa, on McGwire's opposite-field homer

In a game that featured eighth- and ninth-inning grand slams and another blown ninth-inning lead by the Cardinals, McGwire's bases-empty, opposite-field homer was more of an aside. But that doesn't mean it went unnoticed.

The 36,812 McGwire-hungry fans at Busch Stadium took great delight when he drove a pitch from Milwaukee reliever Mike Myers 408 feet to right-center field, completing the Cardinals' scoring in a five-run eighth inning.

Ray Lankford, the batter preceding McGwire, had given the Cardinals a 9-8 lead with a grand slam.

But the Brewers countered with their own rally. The big hit against reliever Rick Croushore in their five-run ninth inning was a grand slam by late-inning defensive replacement Darrin Jackson. It

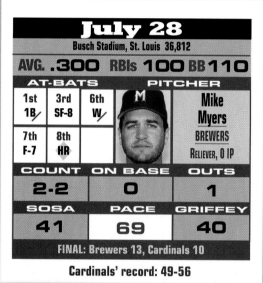

July 28
Busch Stadium, St. Louis 36,812

AVG. .300	RBIs 100	BB 110

AT-BATS

1st 1B /	3rd SF-8	6th W /
7th F-7	8th HR	

PITCHER

Mike Myers
BREWERS
Reliever, 0 IP

COUNT	ON BASE	OUTS
2-2	0	1

SOSA	PACE	GRIFFEY
41	69	40

FINAL: Brewers 13, Cardinals 10

Cardinals' record: 49-56

408 ft.

The ball landed in the right center field seats, just to the left of the Cardinals' bullpen.

marked the seventh time the Cardinals had blown a lead in the ninth inning.

"We were down after those two home runs," Brewers manager Phil Garner said, "but you wouldn't believe how up we were after Darrin's hit."

McGwire's homer was his 25th at Busch Stadium, which tied a team record for home runs at home. Johnny Mize hit 25 of his 43 homers at St. Louis' Sportsman's Park in 1940. McGwire also had a third-inning sacrifice fly and finished the day with 100 RBIs. One walk lifted his major league-leading total to 110.

"I don't want to talk about (the home run)," a subdued McGwire said after the ninth-inning collapse. "This is the way the year's gone. If you want to be a playoff-contending team, you have to win those games."

RUTH *The Babe heated up in a September 6 doubleheader, a splurge that would catapult him toward 60. No. 45 came in the sixth inning of the opener, vs. Boston's Tony Welzer.*

MARIS *After homering in both games of an August 13 doubleheader at Washington, Maris was tied with teammate Mickey Mantle atop the major league home run charts.*

■ "Mark has such discipline of mind. ... He's doing great, he's concentrating great. He doesn't need anyone to give him incentive, he doesn't need a target number. He's really got the perfect focus."
—Cardinals manager Tony La Russa

■ "I know it's tough. Everybody in baseball knows it's tough. I'm just going to give it my best shot." *—McGwire, on hitting home runs*

SLAMMED: *McGwire's 45th home run made a rare appearance in right-center field, but the Brewers got the last laugh in a game that featured two grand slams and a five-run, ninth-inning rally.*

46

"There are more important things to worry about than Mark McGwire hitting home runs. Let's talk about the game."

—McGwire

After seeing his formerly comfortable major league home run lead shrink to two during a season-high 29 at-bat drought, McGwire connected in the fourth inning against Chicago righthander Mark Clark.

But Sammy Sosa, the Cubs right fielder who had taken advantage of Big Mac's slump to close the gap in the homer chase, delivered an in-your-face response with a game-tying, ninth-inning homer. That set the stage for a wild ending to another classic game in the long series between archrivals.

Sosa, who had trailed McGwire 44-38 after games of July 26, continued his surge with a two-run shot off Rick Croushore to force extra innings. The Cubs took leads in both the 11th and 12th innings, but Cardinals Ray Lankford and Eli Marrero answered each

time with tying home runs off closer Rod Beck. Lankford, who had struck out five times in the game before hitting his homer, finally ended the wild affair with a 13th-inning, bases-loaded single.

"I've never seen anything like it," Cardinals manager Tony La Russa said.

"It's one of the greatest games I've ever been associated with," Cubs manager Jim Riggleman said. "They thought they had it and we came back. We thought we had it and they came back."

Lost in the dramatics was another McGwire record—he became the first Cardinals player to homer 26 times at home. McGwire also walked four times, bringing his season total to 119. Sosa, the N.L. leader with 114 RBIs, also singled home the Cubs' go-ahead run in the 12th.

August 8
Busch Stadium, St. Louis 48,064

AVG. .288   RBIs 103   BB 119

AT-BATS

1st F-8	4th HR	6th W
7th W	9th W	11th K
13th W		

PITCHER

Mark Clark
CUBS
STARTER, 6⅓ IP

COUNT ON BASE OUTS
2-1   0   0

| SOSA | PACE | GRIFFEY |
| 44 | 65 | 41 |

FINAL: Cardinals 9, Cubs 8 (13 innings)

Cardinals' record: 55-60

374 ft.

This home run barely reached the first row of Busch Stadium's loge reserved level in left field.

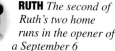 **RUTH** *The second of Ruth's two home runs in the opener of a September 6 doubleheader gave him 46 in 132 games. The victim for both blasts was Boston righthander Tony Welzer.*

 MARIS *Regaining his lead in the home run race, Maris provided the only Yankee scoring in a 2-1 loss to the Chicago White Sox at Yankee Stadium. The August 15 victim was Juan Pizarro.*

■ "It had a little bit of everything. Both Mac and Sammy went deep, and that's what the fans came to see. It was just a fun game to be in." —*Cardinals second baseman Pat Kelly*

■ "When he hits a home run, I'm happy. He was struggling a little and he hadn't had a home run in a long time." —*Sammy Sosa*

47

"I knew when he hit it that it was gone. I turned around and admired it. He hit it a long way."

—Mets pitcher Bobby Jones

McGwire, tied in the home run race with Chicago right fielder Sammy Sosa for about 21 hours, powered a shot off the base of the Busch Stadium scoreboard in left-center to regain the advantage. But the fourth-inning, bases-empty homer could not prevent another lop-sided loss.

After Sosa had pulled into a tie with a two-homer game against San Francisco the night before, Big Mac responded against New York Mets righthander Bobby Jones.

The 464-foot drive gave McGwire the National League record for home runs by the end of August, and he barely missed No. 48 in the sixth

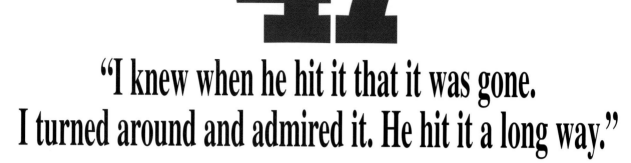

August 11
Busch Stadium, St. Louis 34,489

AVG. .286	RBIs 104	BB 122

AT-BATS			PITCHER
1st 2B⟶	4th HR	6th F-8	**Bobby Jones** METS STARTER, 7 IP
8th K			

COUNT	ON BASE	OUTS
1-0	0	0

SOSA	PACE	GRIFFEY
46	65	41

FINAL: Mets 8, Cardinals 3

Cardinals' record: 56-62

464 ft.

McGwire's 47th homer bounced off the bottom left corner of the Busch Stadium scoreboard sign and landed in the first row of the left field bleachers.

inning when he drove a Jones changeup to the warning track.

"When you pitch against McGwire, you want to move the ball in and out," Jones said. "But it's not like he's not going to hit a home run off you when you pitch him away. He can hit a low pitch and a high pitch. He's so strong that he hits just about everything in the air, no matter where you throw it."

The game was McGwire's 162nd in a Cardinals uniform, the equivalent of a season. The homer was his 71st over that span and his 40th in 81 games at Busch Stadium. He bettered Hack Wilson's N.L. mark for homers by September 1. That was set in 1930, when Wilson had 46 by the end of August.

McGwire's first-inning double ended a streak of 13 plate appearances in which he either had struck out or drawn a base on balls.

 RUTH *Babe ended his three-homer double-header rampage vs. Boston on September 6 with a shot off Jack Russell in the nightcap. It was the ninth of 11 homers he would hit vs. his former team.*

 MARIS *Nos. 47 and 48 came on the afternoon of August 16 at Yankee Stadium vs. Chicago. Lefthander Billy Pierce was the victim both times as Maris completed a stretch of seven homers in six games.*

■ "They booed when I threw him a strike. They booed when I threw him a ball. Strike. Booooo. Ball. Boooo. They just want to see him hit a home run." —*Mets pitcher Al Leiter, on fan reaction when he pitched to McGwire earlier in the series*

48/49

"That's why he's The Man. That's why I keep telling you that Mark McGwire is The Man."

—Sammy Sosa

It was a story right out of scriptwriter's heaven. Cubs vs. Cardinals. Sosa vs. McGwire. A race for baseball immortality.

The 39,689 pumped-up fans who ventured to Wrigley Field for this dramatic showdown involving the Cubs and Cardinals got everything they expected—and more. In the fifth inning, Sosa hit his 48th homer off Cardinals starter Kent Bottenfield, moving past McGwire and into the lead for the first time in the 1998 home run derby and setting off chants of "Sam-mee, Sam-mee" as he circled the bases to a standing ovation.

But the best was yet to come. With his team trailing 6-5 in the eighth, Big Mac responded. He drove a Matt Karchner pitch 430 feet over the left field wall and onto Waveland Avenue, tying the game and reclaiming a share of the home run lead Sosa had held for 58 minutes. Then, in the 10th, McGwire powered a 2-0 Terry Mulholland pitch 402 feet over the center field fence to give the Cardinals a lead they would not relinquish. Challenge accepted.

"Apparently," Cardinals catcher Tom Lampkin said, "the big fellow took it personally."

Before the game, a slumping McGwire had looked tired and confused. But he seemed rejuvenated after his eighth-inning blast. "The last week or so, it was the most frustrated I've ever seen him," said Brian Jordan. "It's been getting to him, everything. The frustration set in. You could see it in his face. It was good to see him relaxed like that."

Juan Acevedo escaped a 10th-inning, bases-loaded jam to pick up the victory.

August 19
Wrigley Field, Chicago 39,689

AVG. **.287**   RBIs **108**   BB **132**

AT-BATS			PITCHER
1st F-7	3rd F-6	5th W/	**Matt Karchner** RELIEVER, 1⅓ IP
6th W/	8th HR	10th HR	**Terry Mulholland** RELIEVER, 2⅔ IP

COUNT	ON BASE	OUTS
3-1, 2-0	0,0	1,1

SOSA	PACE	GRIFFEY
48	64	42

FINAL: Cardinals 8, Cubs 6 (10 innings)

Cardinals' record: 60-64

The first homer sailed over Wrigley's left field fence and onto Waveland Avenue; the second landed in the center field shrubbery.

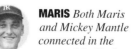

RUTH *Danny Mac-Fayden and Slim Harriss were the victims of another two-homer game at Boston, giving Ruth five homers in two days. His last 24 games would be played at Yankee Stadium.*

MARIS *Both Maris and Mickey Mantle connected in the opener of the Yankees' August 20 doubleheader sweep at Cleveland. Maris retained his three-homer lead with a two-run blast off Jim Perry.*

■ "What a thrill to be at the park as a fan or a teammate to see both those guys come through." —*Cardinals manager Tony La Russa*

■ "Every move we make, every swing we take, every home run we hit. ... he's in the lead, no, he's in the lead. ... it's going to be that way every day till the end of the season." —*McGwire*

WRIGLEY TIME: *As the Sosa-McGwire home run battle heated up, so did the sights and sounds of venerable Wrigley Field. Mac won the unofficial August 19 homer duel, but he didn't diminish the feverish excitement fans were feeling for their resurgent Cubs.*

MARIS METER© SOSA
FROM THE SHORT PORCH IN LEFT

SOSA
21

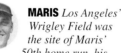

50

"It's ironic breaking Babe's record just right down the street from where he played."

—McGwire

It was an unusual sight. McGwire, epitome of subdued home run trots, pumped his fist into the air and clapped twice before he'd touched second base.

He punched his fist into the air again as he approached the plate and yet again before disappearing into the dugout. But even after he'd vanished, a standing ovation continued at Shea Stadium.

The reason for Big Mac's exuberance: home run No. 50, a modest 369-footer that loomed large in historical significance.

The drive over the left field wall gave him a distinction no other player in baseball history can claim. McGwire became the first to hit 50 or more home runs in three consecutive seasons, breaking the record he shared with Babe Ruth. The moment was not lost on him.

"Obviously, it's history,"

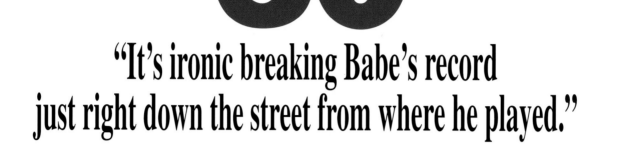

August 20

Shea Stadium, New York 45,308

AVG. .286	RBIs 109	BB 132

AT-BATS			PITCHER
1st K	4th F-5	7th HR	Willie Blair
9th F-8			METS STARTER, 7 IP

COUNT	ON BASE	OUTS
2-1	0	0

SOSA	PACE	GRIFFEY
48	65	42

FINAL: Cardinals 2, Mets 0

Cardinals' record: 61-64

369 ft.

McGwire hit his 50th home run into the bottom left corner of Shea Stadium's left center field bleachers.

McGwire said. "First baseball player to do it three consecutive years. There's been thousands of power hitters to play this game, and nobody's ever done it. ... And I'm pretty proud of it."

McGwire's seventh-inning home run, off Willie Blair, followed a solo shot by teammate Brian Jordan and provided all the scoring Donovan Osborne and Juan Acevedo would need for their four-hit shutout in the opener of a doubleheader.

McGwire, who became the oldest player to reach the 50-homer plateau at 34 years, 324 days, had been 2-for-16 with nine strikeouts vs. Blair entering the game.

"I just made a mistake," Blair said. "I've gotten him out a lot on that pitch (slider). But that one wasn't where I wanted it."

RUTH *Babe's September 11 solo home run was his 50th of the season and his fourth off St. Louis Browns righthander Milt Gaston. Ruth reached the homestretch in the Yankees' 138th game.*

MARIS *Los Angeles' Wrigley Field was the site of Maris' 50th home run, his first off Angels' righthander Ken McBride. Maris made the turn on August 22, in his team's 125th game.*

■ "I'd like to see him break the record. I think he deserves it. He respects the game. He works hard." *—Mets pitcher Willie Blair*

■ "It was almost like a relief. I got to 49 and you need one more, and it can take some time to get that extra one. This time it took only one day. It was a relief." *—McGwire*

■ "I have to thank the fans here in New York. It was tremendous. I mean, wow, what a reception!" *—McGwire*

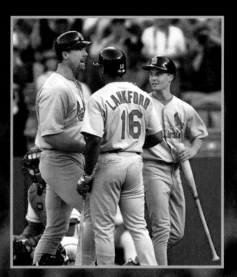

HAPPY 50TH:
After becoming the first player in history to hit 50 home runs in three consecutive years, McGwire stayed up half the night signing special 50-50-50 balls for teammates and others associated with the team.

50·50·50
8·20·98

51

"He (10-year-old son Matt) was the first person I called. But he already knew."

—McGwire

Rejuvenated and suddenly ready to focus on the record he had been reluctant to discuss for much of the season, McGwire punctuated 4 hours 44 minutes of baseball at Shea Stadium with his second homer of the day and 51st of the season.

Having hit his record-setting 50th homer in a Cardinals' victory in the opener of a doubleheader against the Mets, McGwire went deep again in the nightcap. In his first-inning at-bat against righthander Rick Reed, he smashed a 385-foot drive that bounced off of the left field foul pole. His fourth home run in seven at-bats over a two-day

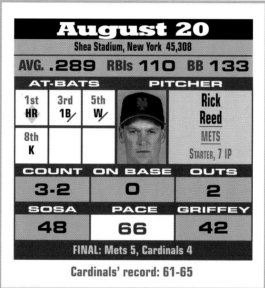

August 20

Shea Stadium, New York 45,308

AVG. .289	RBIs 110	BB 133

AT-BATS			PITCHER
1st HR	3rd 1B	5th W	**Rick Reed** METS STARTER, 7 IP
8th K			

COUNT	ON BASE	OUTS
3-2	0	2

SOSA	PACE	GRIFFEY
48	66	42

FINAL: Mets 5, Cardinals 4

Cardinals' record: 61-65

Homer No. 51 bounced off Shea Stadium's left field foul pole, about 15 feet above the first row of seats.

span gave the Cardinals an early lead in a game they eventually would lose.

After the doubleheader, fulfilling a promise he had been making all season, McGwire discussed his prospects of breaking Roger Maris' single-season home run record.

"I have to say I do have a good shot," he said. "But I know it's going to be tough. I truly believe that if someone gets to 50 by September 1, they have a legitimate shot down the stretch run."

McGwire, who had hit career homer No. 400 earlier in the season off Reed, pulled three home runs ahead of Chicago right fielder Sammy Sosa. And McGwire created a different kind of excitement in the third inning of Game 2 when he stole his first base of the season, the 11th of his 13-year career and his third with the Cardinals.

 RUTH *A two-run homer off Cleveland righthander Willis Hudlin got Ruth off to a good start in the opener of what would become a festive September 13 doubleheader at Yankee Stadium.*

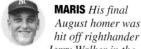 **MARIS** *His final August homer was hit off righthander Jerry Walker in the sixth inning vs. the A's at Kansas City. He moved five homers ahead of Mickey Mantle in the great home run chase.*

■ "I had no problem with what they (the fans) did. If we win, he can hit all the home runs he wants. I'd cheer, too, if I was one of them." —*Mets pitcher Rick Reed*

■ "I've got my second wind." —*McGwire*

52

"I'm just going to try and enjoy what's going on. I don't know if I'll ever be in this situation again."

—McGwire

Onward and upward. Having shaken an early-August dry spell, McGwire continued a relentless record march with a towering 477-foot homer off Francisco Cordova in a lopsided loss to the Pirates.

The game seemed to be secondary for 45,082 fans who filled many seats that usually go unoccupied at Three Rivers Stadium.

McGwire delivered for them in the first inning, when he hit a Cordova pitch into the stands in right-center. It was his third opposite-field homer of the season.

"That was by accident, believe me," McGwire said. "I

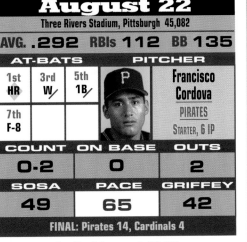

August 22

Three Rivers Stadium, Pittsburgh 45,082

AVG. .292	RBIs 112	BB 135

AT-BATS			PITCHER
1st HR	3rd W/	5th 1B/	Francisco Cordova
7th F-8			PIRATES STARTER, 6 IP

COUNT	ON BASE	OUTS
0-2	0	2

SOSA	PACE	GRIFFEY
49	65	42

FINAL: Pirates 14, Cardinals 4

Cardinals' record: 62-67

The ball went over Three Rivers Stadium's right center field fence and disappeared into a sea of screaming fans.

wasn't sure if I'd hit it hard enough. Last weekend, I was guessing against (Cordova) too much, so I just tried to react to the ball."

The home run, the fifth in McGwire's last 14 at-bats, was greeted by a standing ovation—much louder than any the Pirates received. The reaction was hard to ignore.

"Oh, yeah, you can feel it," McGwire said. "It takes me off guard when you hear it on the road. I don't think any visiting player is used to playing before different crowds, all of them cheering for you."

The homer was Mac's 162nd over three seasons, moving him one ahead of Babe Ruth's three-season record set in 1926-28. The 52 total equaled the third-highest total in N.L. history and the most by a National Leaguer since George Foster hit that many in 1977.

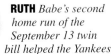

RUTH *Babe's second home run of the September 13 twin bill helped the Yankees complete their sweep of Cleveland and clinch the A.L. pennant. Joe Shaute became a three-time victim.*

MARIS *The Yankee right fielder continued his march by posting his seventh multihomer game of the season. His first homer in the September 2 game was hit off Detroit's Frank Lary.*

■ "I would think that a majority of America is watching. To know that every eye in the country, every eye in the stadium is watching, and every move that you make is critiqued, that's pressure. But I'll deal with it." —*McGwire*

■ "The buzz is so alive, so real, you can almost touch it. I just want to listen. And then you look into the stands, and you see the look of joy on all those faces." —*Cardinals manager Tony La Russa*

53

"I guarantee you that 47,000 people didn't come out to see me play baseball here today."

—Pirates first baseman Kevin Young

The snowballing magnetism of McGwire mania rolled through Pittsburgh, leaving normally hard-to-impress Pirates fans gasping in the wake of another Big Mac power surge. McGwire's 1998 home run parade inspired the first consecutive regular-season sell-outs in the 28-year history of Three Rivers Stadium—and the Cardinals' big first baseman didn't disappoint.

Moments after Cubs rival Sammy Sosa had hit homer 50 against Houston in Chicago, and minutes before Sosa would connect again for 51, McGwire drove an eighth-inning pitch from lefthander Ricardo Rincon 393 feet into the left field seats and joined Hack Wilson and Ralph Kiner as the only N.L. players to hit as many as 53 homers in a season.

The Pittsburgh crowd roared as McGwire circled the bases

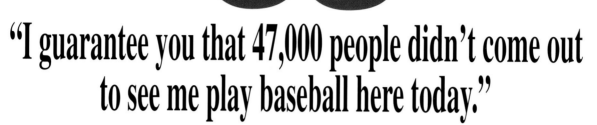

August 23
Three Rivers Stadium, Pittsburgh 42,134

AVG. .295	RBIs 113	BB 137

AT-BATS			PITCHER	
1st 6-3	3rd W	5th 2B		Ricardo Rincon
6th W	8th HR			PIRATES Reliever, 1⅓ IP

COUNT	ON BASE	OUTS
2-2	0	2

SOSA	PACE	GRIFFEY
51	66	43

FINAL: Pirates 4, Cardinals 3

Cardinals' record: 62-68

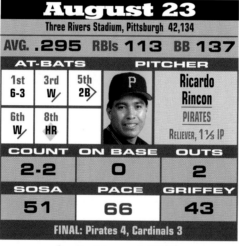

Pittsburgh fans got another Mac souvenir when homer 53 landed in the seats just above the fence in left field.

and returned to the dugout. But as the cheering picked up steam, teammates nudged him back onto the field for a rare honor—an opposing-park curtain call.

"When a crowd responds like that, the professional thing to do is acknowledge it," said Cardinals manager Tony La Russa. "He wasn't kicking and screaming, but he wasn't going to do it without being reminded."

McGwire's sixth homer in five days came amid a controversy over his use of androstenedione, a legal testosterone-producing, strength-enhancing substance that is permitted by baseball. It also came in a losing cause as the Pirates won their seventh straight game.

McGwire extended his own record for home runs by a righthanded batter over two seasons to 111.

 RUTH *A homer off Ted Blankenship in the third inning propelled the Yankees to a 7-2 victory in the September 16 opener of a five-game sweep of Chicago. With 11 games remaining, Ruth had 53.*

 **MARIS** *A two-run, eighth-inning blow off Detroit's Hank Aguirre capped Maris' two-homer September 2 game and gave him 53 home runs with 28 games remaining on the Yankees' schedule.*

■ "He deserves that ovation, and he deserves to be able to come out like that. He's chasing history, and we won the ballgame. It worked out fine. I didn't mind it." —*Pirates catcher Jason Kendall*

■ "I felt uncomfortable doing that (making a curtain call) as a visiting player, in all due respect for the Pirates. But a couple of teammates said I should go out there, so I did." —*McGwire*

MAN OF STEEL: *All eyes (bottom photo) watch the flight of home run 53, a special treat for McGwire-crazy fans who packed Pittsburgh's Three Rivers Stadium on consecutive days.*

54

"I can only take care of myself. Let's just have fun watching until the end of the season."

—McGwire, on his battle with Sammy Sosa

McGwire's eighth-inning home run was a thing of beauty. What happened thereafter to the Cardinals was not—at least in the view of McGwire and 30,004 stunned fans at Busch Stadium.

Big Mac stepped into a pitch from Florida Marlins rookie Justin Speier and sent a majestic drive that bounced off the top of the 35-foot backdrop in center field. The 509-footer was his fourth home run of the season at Busch Stadium that measured more than 500 feet.

The home run extended the Cardinals' lead to 3-0 and seemingly unnerved Speier, who served up a three-run homer to John Mabry later in the inning.

But the celebrating was short-lived. Florida's Derrek Lee, Cliff Floyd and Kevin Orie hit consecutive ninth-inning

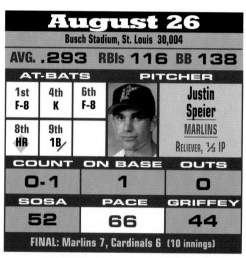

August 26

Busch Stadium, St. Louis 30,004

AVG. **.293** RBIs **116** BB **138**

AT-BATS			PITCHER
1st F-8	4th K	6th F-8	**Justin Speier**
8th HR	9th 1B/		MARLINS RELIEVER, ⅓ IP

COUNT	ON BASE	OUTS
0-1	1	0

SOSA	PACE	GRIFFEY
52	66	44

FINAL: Marlins 7, Cardinals 6 (10 innings)

Cardinals' record: 62-70

509 ft.

This majestic drive to straightaway center field bounced off the top of Busch Stadium's 35-foot backdrop.

homers off reliever John Frascatore, and pinch-hitter Mark Kotsay tied the game with a three-run blow off Jeff Brantley. The Marlins won the game in the 10th on Randy Knorr's double.

"I'm not even sure what I saw," Cardinals manager Tony La Russa said. "I certainly don't know how to describe it. Pretty horrible."

McGwire called the emotional swing "probably one of the worst I've ever had in my career." But the media focus continued to be the great home run chase that had heated up earlier in the day, when Chicago right fielder Sammy Sosa hit No. 52.

"I know what America is watching," a disappointed McGwire conceded. "They're not watching the Cardinals, they're watching me. And that's hard to accept."

RUTH *Homer No. 54 was hit off Chicago's Ted Lyons in the second game of a September 18 doubleheader. Lyons was the first of two future Hall of Famers who would serve up Ruth homers.*

MARIS *Washington righthander Tom Cheney became Maris victim No. 54 on September 6 in a game at Yankee Stadium. The blow gave Maris a three-homer lead over teammate Mickey Mantle.*

■ "I wouldn't want to be in his shoes day in and day out. Personally, I wouldn't like all that attention. It takes a special person to handle it." *—Marlins third baseman Kevin Orie*

■ "I knew it was gone. You want to challenge a hitter like him and go right after him, and if he hits one off you, oh well." *—Marlins pitcher Justin Speier*

FOLLOW THE BOUNCING BALL: *That's what Marlins reliever Justin Speier was doing (above) after McGwire bounced a 509-foot shot off the backdrop in straightaway center field at Busch Stadium for home run No. 54.*

The ejection

Somewhere between home runs 54 and 55, McGwire lost his patience and St. Louis fans threw a nationally televised temper tantrum.

The August 29 game at Busch Stadium against the Atlanta Braves was devoid of McGwire home runs, but not of the fireworks that normally follow his at-bats. Big Mac took a Saturday afternoon off from the Great Home Run Chase and reminded the world that he is indeed human.

The game got off to a temperamental start when McGwire took a called third strike from pitcher Tom Glavine, a pitch that appeared low and inside to the big first baseman. He questioned umpire Sam Holbrook's judgment and when the conversation became animated, manager Tony La Russa and third base coach Rene Lachemann rushed to intercede.

But McGwire, restrained by Lachemann, refused to back off and was ejected, along with La Russa and coach Dave Duncan. The ejection was not accepted gracefully by the capacity crowd, which tossed considerable debris onto the field—prompting a threat of forfeit. Peace was restored and McGwire had an afternoon off, courtesy of Holbrook.

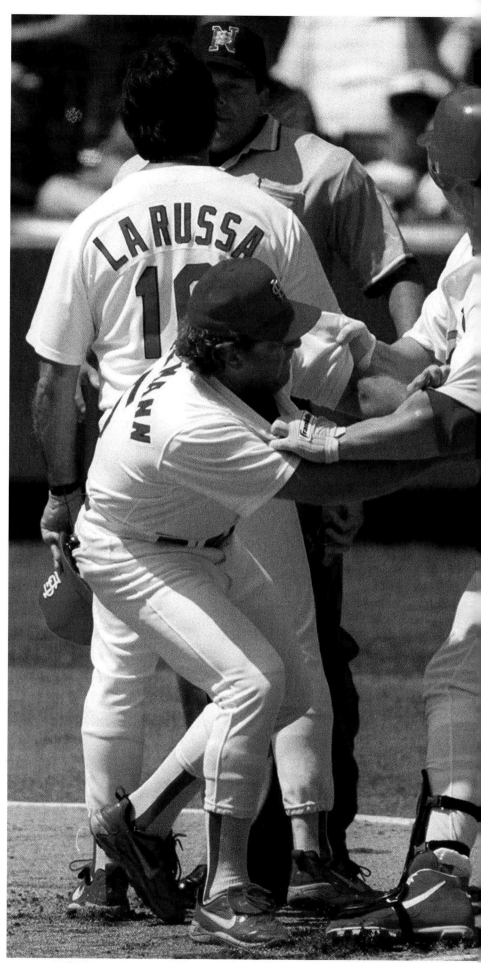

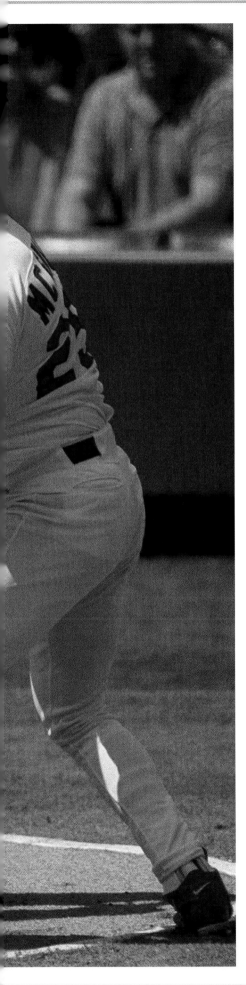

OUT PATTERN:
As McGwire (above) argues with Holbrook, LaRussa nears the plate and Lachemann runs up the third-base line. Lachemann's attempts to restrain Mac couldn't stop the ejection.

55

"This is a Mark McGwire show. No matter what happened, I believe he's going to come back—as always."

—Chicago's Sammy Sosa, after tying McGwire briefly at 54 home runs

Like two great boxers looking for a late-round knockout, Mac and Sammy continued to jab and counterpunch their way through the myth and legend that surrounds one of baseball's most cherished feats.

Reflecting a pattern of the previous two weeks, Chicago right fielder Sammy Sosa hit his 54th home run in an afternoon game at Colorado, tying him with McGwire for the major league lead. But Mac answered with a game-winning, three-run blast against the Atlanta Braves in a Sunday night game at St. Louis. It marked the third straight McGwire home run that had come on the same day as Sosa homers.

"I've said it time and time again. I can only take care of Mark McGwire, period," McGwire said after his

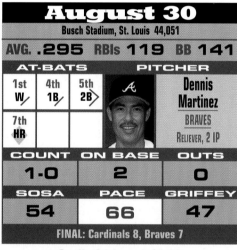

August 30

Busch Stadium, St. Louis 44,051

AVG. .295	RBIs 119	BB 141

AT-BATS			PITCHER
1st W/	4th 1B/	5th 2B▷	Dennis Martinez
7th HR			BRAVES
			RELIEVER, 2 IP

COUNT	ON BASE	OUTS
1-0	2	0

SOSA	PACE	GRIFFEY
54	66	47

FINAL: Cardinals 8, Braves 7

Cardinals' record: 64-72

501 ft.

The latest McGwire cannon shot fell between the backdrop and Coke bottle sign in straightaway center field.

dramatic seventh-inning homer had completed the Cardinals' comeback from a 6-0 deficit. "This is not a challenge, this is not a race to whatever. We don't get an Oscar at the end for like best actor. He takes care of himself, I take care of myself and wherever the chips fall at the end of the season, that's where it is."

McGwire's 501-foot shot to center field off veteran righthander Dennis Martinez came the day after he had been ejected in the first inning of a nationally televised game against the Braves for arguing a called third strike.

The homer moved McGwire past former Pittsburgh star Ralph Kiner into second place on the National League's single-season home run charts. He needed only one more to match the 1930 record of Chicago Cubs outfielder Hack Wilson.

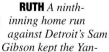

RUTH *A ninth-inning home run against Detroit's Sam Gibson kept the Yankees from suffering their first home shutout loss of the season. Homer No. 55 came September 21 in the team's 148th game.*

MARIS *Continuing a run of five homers in nine games, Maris belted his 55th on September 7 vs. Cleveland's Dick Stigman at Yankee Stadium. After 141 games, he was five short of Ruth's record.*

■ "Sammy always says I'm The Man. But he's The Man, too. He's right there. I was asked today, 'What if we both finish up with over 62?' What can you do except say what a great year? A historical year. I mean, there's a good possibility that might happen." —*McGwire*

■ "I'm extremely happy for Sammy. Sammy is having a magical year, a way better year than I'm having. His team is right there in the wild-card race, he's driven in quite a few more runs than I have, he's hit for a higher average. You tip your hat to him." —*McGwire*

55 AND COUNTING:
The Atlanta Braves and veteran righthander Dennis Martinez got 'McGwired' in a nationally televised Sunday night game at Busch Stadium. Big Mac ignited the crowd with a three-run, seventh-inning blast that carried the Cardinals to a dramatic come-from-behind victory.

56/57

"The bat felt pretty good tonight. America is watching very closely. It's become enjoyable, and it's become fun."

—McGwire

After 68 years and a host of unsuccessful challenges, Hack Wilson finally surrendered his National League single-season home run record, giving way to that man named McGwire.

The Cardinals' first baseman scarcely had time to savor the moment after blasting a Livan Hernandez pitch 450 feet in the seventh inning. The homer, McGwire's 56th, traveled into the tarp-covered center field seats at Florida's Pro Player Stadium.

Two innings later, he hit the first pitch from reliever Donn Pall into the same area, a 472-footer for record-setting homer No. 57 as the Cardinals eased past the Marlins.

"It's a pretty awesome feat," McGwire acknowledged. "I didn't realize till the other day that (56) was the record. Almost everybody in the dugout congratulated me and hugged

me, and the fans here in south Florida gave me two curtain calls, which is unbelievable."

In his rapid-fire move past Wilson, McGwire answered another Sammy Sosa challenge. Sosa, the Chicago right fielder, had hit his 55th home run one day earlier and entered the Cubs' night game against Cincinnati tied with McGwire. But Sosa went 0-for-4 while Big Mac was making history.

"I think one of the reasons he is going to do it (break Roger Maris' record) is because I'm right there with him," Sosa said. "He is a competitive guy, and I think he responds to a challenge."

The multihomer game was McGwire's seventh of the season and 50th of his career.

Ray Lankford and Ron Gant also homered for the Cardinals, and Matt Morris pitched five-hit ball over seven innings.

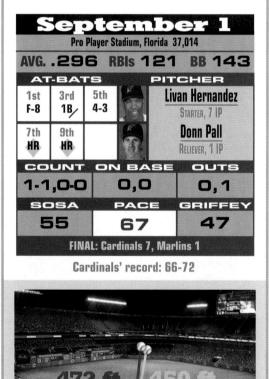

September 1
Pro Player Stadium, Florida 37,014

AVG. **.296** RBIs **121** BB **143**

AT-BATS			PITCHER
1st F-8	3rd 1B/	5th 4-3	**Livan Hernandez** STARTER, 7 IP
7th HR	9th HR		**Donn Pall** RELIEVER, 1 IP

COUNT	ON BASE	OUTS
1-1,0-0	0,0	0,1

SOSA	PACE	GRIFFEY
55	67	47

FINAL: Cardinals 7, Marlins 1

Cardinals' record: 66-72

McGwire's two home runs landed within a few feet of each other on a tarp that covered seats in straightaway center field.

RUTH *A September 27 grand slam off future Hall of Famer Lefty Grove touched off the closing four-homers-in-three-games surge that lifted the Bambino to his season total of 60.*

MARIS *A September 16 two-run shot off Detroit righthander Frank Lary ended Maris' seven-game homerless drought and brought his record-chasing total to 57 with 12 games remaining.*

■ "He's going to do it. He's going to get the record, and I think everyone knows he's going to do it now. This is an incredible man." —*Cardinals catcher Tom Lampkin*

■ "I've never seen anything like this in my life. I saw Nolan Ryan win his 300th game, and throw two no-hitters, and get his 5,000th strikeout, but this is unbelievable what (McGwire's) doing. He just gets people so excited. He's like a movie star and a rock 'n' roll star rolled into one." —*Cardinals pitcher Bobby Witt*

HACKING AWAY:
McGwire Mania hit record heights during an eventful trip to Florida when he struck twice in a game against the Marlins and claimed the N.L. single-season homer mark previously held by Chicago's Hack Wilson (right).

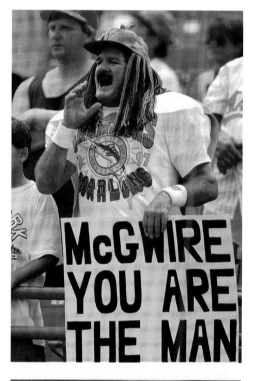

TWO PLUS TWO: *The sign (below) relayed the feeling of Marlins fans for McGwire, who delivered with his second two-homer salvo in as many days at Florida's Pro Player Stadium. He returned to St. Louis and Busch Stadium on the brink of history.*

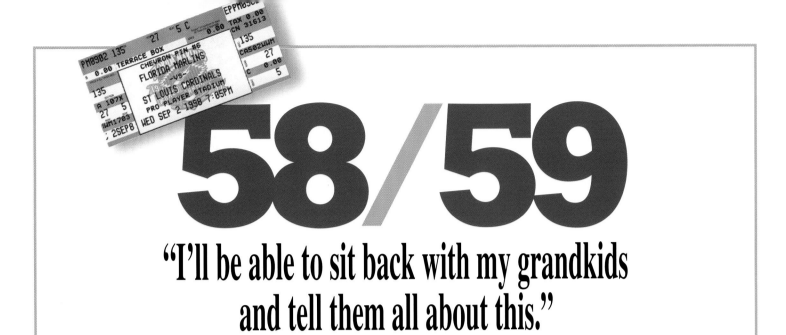

58/59

"I'll be able to sit back with my grandkids and tell them all about this."

—*Cardinals second baseman Delino DeShields*

With two more flicks of his powerful wrists, McGwire crossed into territory charted by only two players among the more than 15,000 who have played the game. After pushing Hack Wilson to the sideline with a dramatic two-homer effort the previous night, Big Mac did the same to Jimmie Foxx and Hank Greenberg with a Herculean two-homer encore at Florida's Pro Player Stadium. After the game, only Babe Ruth and Roger Maris stood between McGwire and what appeared to be his destiny.

McGwire's second consecutive two-homer night followed script. In becoming the most prolific single-season home run hitter in National League history the night before, he connected in the seventh and ninth innings. Home runs 58 and 59 were hit to left and left-center in the seventh and eighth, the

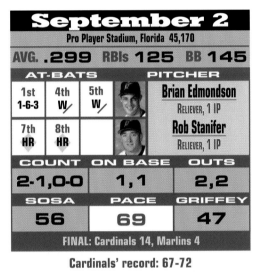

September 2
Pro Player Stadium, Florida 45,170

AVG. .299	RBIs 125	BB 145

AT-BATS			PITCHER
1st 1-6-3	4th W/	5th W/	**Brian Edmondson** RELIEVER, 1 IP
7th HR	8th HR		**Rob Stanifer** RELIEVER, 1 IP

COUNT	ON BASE	OUTS
2-1,0-0	1,1	2,2

SOSA	PACE	GRIFFEY
56	69	47

FINAL: Cardinals 14, Marlins 4

Cardinals' record: 67-72

497 ft.
458 ft

McGwire's first homer was an upper-deck shot to left; his second went into the lower deck in left center at Pro Player Stadium.

first a 497-foot, upper-deck shot off rookie Brian Edmondson and the second a first-pitch 458-footer off Rob Stanifer.

"What's going on is pretty big," McGwire conceded after making two more curtain calls for a large Florida crowd. "It's quite amazing. It almost blows me away."

McGwire's second straight big night helped ensure an easy victory that also featured pitcher Kent Mercker's fourth-inning grand slam. His encore effort answered another challenge by Chicago's Sammy Sosa, who had homered for the 56th time earlier in the day. On the single-season chart, McGwire moved past Foxx, Greenberg and McGwire himself—all of whom had hit 58—and into a tie with Ruth, who hit 59 in 1921.

McGwire left Florida with 12 homers in a 17-game span.

RUTH *Hod Lisenbee and Paul Hopkins, two Washington righthanders, served up homers 58 and 59 to Ruth in his second-last game of the season. No. 59 was his second grand slam in two games.*

MARIS *Creeping ever closer to his destiny, Maris hit No. 58 against Detroit and 59 against Baltimore in a four-day span. His September 20 blow off Milt Pappas came in New York's 155th game.*

■ "The pitch was probably three inches off the ground. I amazed myself that I went down and got it." —*McGwire, on his 58th homer*

■ "He crushed it. It's amazing. You can't throw the guy any pitch he can reach or he hits it 500 feet. It's a little unfair at times. He's like the Michael Jordan of baseball." —*Marlins pitcher Rob Stanifer on homer No. 59*

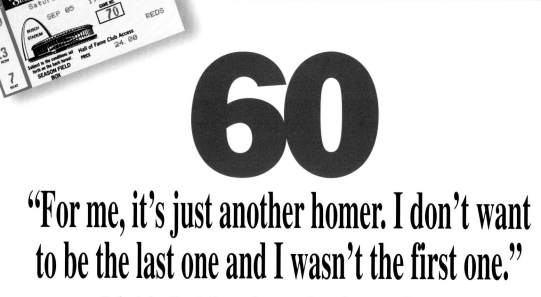

St. Louis Cardinals
12:15PM
Saturday
SEP 05 1998
GAME NO. 70
VS
REDS
160
SEC.
13
ROW
7
SEAT
BUSCH STADIUM
Hall of Fame Club Access
24.00
PRICE
Subject to the conditions set forth on the back hereof.
SEASON FIELD BOX

60

"For me, it's just another homer. I don't want to be the last one and I wasn't the first one."

——Reds pitcher Dennis Reyes, after surrendering homer No. 60 to McGwire

It started as an over-hyped dream in January and became an early-September reality.

When McGwire launched a 2-0 fastball from Cincinnati lefthander Dennis Reyes into Busch Stadium's left field seats, he took his place alongside Babe Ruth and Roger Maris as the only 60-home run bashers in history.

McGwire achieved the 60-homer plateau, a standard by which sluggers have been measured since Ruth hit that many in 1927, on his first swing of a festive Saturday afternoon. The high drive sailed just inside the foul pole and sent a crowd of 47,994 into a prolonged roar.

Big Mac's homer gave the Cardinals a 2-0 lead, and Donovan Osborne secured a Cardinals win with a three-hit shutout that was witnessed by numerous baseball dignitaries and more than 700 media mem-

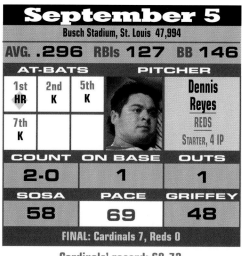

September 5

Busch Stadium, St. Louis 47,994

AVG. .296	RBIs 127	BB 146

AT-BATS			PITCHER	
1st HR	2nd K	5th K	**Dennis Reyes** REDS STARTER, 4 IP	
7th K				

COUNT	ON BASE	OUTS
2-0	1	1

SOSA	PACE	GRIFFEY
58	69	48

FINAL: Cardinals 7, Reds 0

Cardinals' record: 68-73

381 ft.

Historic home run No. 60 disappeared into the seats just inside the left field foul pole.

bers from around the world.

McGwire stepped onto the Ruthian plateau in the team's 142nd game, 12 fewer than Ruth needed to reach 60. And he got there against the only National League team that had not surrendered a home run to him in 1998. Against Reds pitching, Big Mac had managed two singles in 16 previous at-bats, with 12 walks.

As he moved one swing shy of Maris' 1961 record of 61, McGwire surpassed his wildest expectations. "Babe Ruth," he repeated over and over. "You are almost speechless when people put your name alongside his."

Despite McGwire's historic effort, the shadow of Chicago right fielder Sammy Sosa remained. Hours after Big Mac had hit his 60th homer, Sosa recorded his 58th, in Three Rivers Stadium at Pittsburgh.

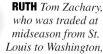

RUTH *Tom Zachary, who was traded at midseason from St. Louis to Washington, joined Ruth in the record books when he served up home run No. 60 in the Babe's 154th and final regular-season game.*

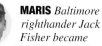

MARIS *Baltimore righthander Jack Fisher became Maris' 60th victim September 26 in the third inning of a game at Yankee Stadium. The record-tying homer was hit in game No. 159.*

■ "Let's just accept what is happening, enjoy it, ride the wave. I mean, look what it has done to baseball. If you want to say it has brought America together, it has." —*McGwire*

■ "He motivates me. I motivate him. And this is fun. ... We're pushing each other. We're not going to stop now. We're doing a great job together." —*Cubs right fielder Sammy Sosa*

"One day, we will meet."

The discomfort of an early-September heat wave couldn't diminish the happiness and harmony that filled Busch Stadium. And while the temperature for Cardinals game No. 142 hovered in the mid-90s, the degree of fan and player

anticipation rose to a feverish pitch.

Every McGwire move, every gesture, every expression was cheered with an almost-religious fervor while being chronicled for posterity. As more than 700 media representatives prepared to analyze shots that would be heard around the world, millions of fans were brought to attention by radio and television announcers who dared compare the challenger to baseball's ultimate

heavyweight: Babe Ruth.

Yes, the immortal Babe Ruth, who had blasted his way through the 1920s and into the record book with a 60-homer 1927 season, setting a standard by which future generations of sluggers would be measured.

And when McGwire brought down the house with a first-inning swing that sent the baseball world into an uncontrollable spin, the sanctity of the Ruthian accomplishment and the torment suffered by Roger Maris, the only previous challenger to match Ruth's 60 homers, was not lost on the Cardinals first baseman.

"I truly believe that ... they're both watching," McGwire said after home run No. 60 in a Cardinals' victory over Cincinnati. "I can feel it. And one day, we will meet."

Their paths crossed in the record books on McGwire's first at-bat. Responding to the standing, roaring ovations that had greeted his every at-bat since home run No. 59, he touched off a citywide celebration with a high drive that settled comfortably into the seats just inside the left field foul pole.

As the normally low-key McGwire made a fist-pumping trot around the bases, ecstatic fans hugged, leaped and danced in Busch Stadium's aisles and living rooms throughout the country.

They were participating in the magic of McGwire while paying tribute to the glory of Ruth.

"Obviously, he was the most important sports figure in the world of that time," said McGwire, who moved two swings away from one of the most cherished records in sports. "Babe Ruth. What can you say? You are almost speechless when people put your name alongside his name.

"I wish I could go back in time and meet him. Hopefully when I pass away, I'll get to meet him and then I can truly find out what he was really like."

SEEING RED: *Interested observers of homer No. 60 included St. Louis Hall of Famers Red Schoendienst and Stan Musial, who serenaded fans on his harmonica. Reds pitcher Dennis Reyes was not in a celebratory mood after serving up the record-tying blast.*

61

"That's storybook stuff. ... And he actually did it. It's like Star Wars, with Luke (Skywalker). The Force was with him."

—Cardinals left fielder Ron Gant

The missile descended at 1:22 p.m., a split second after banging off the glass that protected diners in the Stadium Club, located between the upper and lower decks in left field at Busch Stadium.

As it disappeared into a sea of Cardinal red, so did the last vestiges of doubt about McGwire's assault on one of baseball's most cherished records.

"It's been a long, rough road," McGwire said after his 61st home run, a solo shot in the first inning, matched the 37-year-old, single-season record of Roger Maris. "I go back to, I don't know, January, talking about it into spring training, and here we are, tied at 61. I am one swing away from breaking it."

The 430-foot blast off of Chicago righthander Mike Morgan moved McGwire past

September 7

Busch Stadium, St. Louis 50,530

AVG. .296	RBIs 128	BB 147

AT-BATS			PITCHER	
1st HR	3rd 1B	5th F-8		Mike Morgan
7th F-8				CUBS STARTER, 6 IP

COUNT	ON BASE	OUTS
1-1	0	2

SOSA	PACE	GRIFFEY
58	69	50

FINAL: Cardinals 3, Cubs 2

Cardinals' record: 70-73

430 ft.

The record-tying home run bounced off a Stadium Club window just inside the left field foul pole and landed in the first row of loge reserved seats.

another former Yankee, Babe Ruth, on the single-season home run chart. Ruth needed 154 games to hit 60 in 1927; McGwire needed only 144 to hit 61. Maris hit his 61st on the final day of the 1961 season, the team's 163rd game.

The home run was doubly sweet because it helped the Cardinals defeat longtime rival Chicago. And Big Mac's primary challenger, Sammy Sosa, watched the historic moment from his position in right field. Later, after Sosa had singled, he hugged McGwire in a touching scene at first base.

After McGwire hit Morgan's third pitch, he stood near the plate, watched the ball leave the park in fair territory and began his record-tying celebration. "As soon as it left my bat, I just threw my hands up," McGwire said. "I knew it at that time. What a feeling that was."

MARIS *Homer 61, which made Maris the greatest single-season slugger in baseball history, was hit in New York's 163rd and final game, an October 1 victory over Boston at Yankee Stadium. The history-making pitch was served up by Tracy Stallard.*

■ "This guy is doing everything, isn't he? It's like I've always said. He's a better person than he is a player." *—Cardinals manager Tony La Russa*

■ "It has been quite amazing. I think I have amazed myself. I think I have amazed other people. So it is hard not to have emotions for this." *—McGwire*

■ "I told him that I got to 61, so he should be able to do it, too." *—John McGwire, who was celebrating his 61st birthday when Mark hit homer No. 61*

"Swing and look at there! Look at there! Look at there! McGwire's No. 61! McGwire's Flight 61 headed for planet Maris! Home run McGwire, 61. ... Pardon me while I stand and applaud."

—The historic 61st-homer call from Hall of Fame broadcaster Jack Buck

A family affair

It was the birthday bash of the century, but few of the celebrants even knew that's what it was. But, oh, what a present!

"I didn't call him today to say happy birthday, because I was driving to the ballpark," McGwire said. "I said this is meant to be his birthday present. Sixty-first home run on his 61st birthday. Happy birthday, Dad! I mean, you can't ask for anything better than that."

John McGwire got the message, loud and clear. It was delivered with a first-inning crack of the bat

ALL IN THE FAMILY: *Birthday boy John McGwire (left) got a special gift from son Mark—homer No. 61 on birthday No. 61. Mac also enjoyed a home-plate family reunion (right photo) with son Matt and a postgame hug (above) with the children of Roger Maris, whose record he matched.*

that echoed through the baseball world and lifted his son onto the 61-homer plateau previously occupied by only Roger Maris. The message was reinforced by a triumphant home run trot that punctuated his son's ascension to record heights, followed by a birthday salute into the stands.

The wild, emotional celebration, played out in front of 50,530 raucous Busch Stadium fans and a national television audience, was very much a family affair.

After receiving congratulatory slaps and bashes from Cubs Mark Grace and Gary Gaetti and Cardinals coach Rene Lachemann and center fielder Ray Lankford during a fist-pumping romp around the bases, Mark McGwire looked down into the wide eyes of his 10-year-old son, who had arrived from his southern California home in the first inning.

"I didn't see him there in the top of the first inning," McGwire said. "I went to the hole to get my bat and

PLAY IT AGAIN, SAMMY: *Seven innings after his 61st homer, McGwire and Chicago's Sammy Sosa enjoyed an impromptu celebration at first base.*

there he is. I told him I loved him. I gave him a kiss."

And then, after circling the bases, he gave young Matt a bear hug and carried him halfway to the dugout. "Next thing I knew I see him at home plate and what a wonderful feeling a father could have."

McGwire also attended to the business of another family with an emotional salute to the children of Roger Maris, who were seated along the first-base line. "I pointed to my heart and said, 'Roger's with me,'" McGwire said. "I would love to meet with them some day when this is all over and tell them the feeling what their father was going through at the time because it is an amazing feeling."

A feeling that will never go away.

"I don't think you ever let go of the moment," McGwire said. "I don't know if I'll ever be here again, so how can you let it go? What I've done is fabulous. I'm going to enjoy it right now. The whole time, I just thought, 'What a great birthday present for my father.'"

62

"It was a sweet, sweet run around the bases. ... I hope I didn't act foolish, but this was history."

——McGwire, after his record-breaking home run

It was a line drive into the corner, not your average, everyday McGwire production. The 341-foot shot barely cleared the wall, well below the lower left field seats, and fell unmolested into a storage area below the stands.

Ordinarily, Big Mac might have been tempted to throw this minnow back. But on this special night at Busch Stadium, everything was a keeper.

62!

The number flashed through the minds of baseball fans throughout the world as McGwire made one of the most memorable and historic home run trots in the game's history. He missed first base and had to return to the scene of the crime. He bashed, mashed and hugged everybody in sight, friends and opponents alike. He danced, he jumped, he yelled and he celebrated the

September 8

Busch Stadium, St. Louis 49,987

AVG. **.297** RBIs **129** BB **149**

AT-BATS			PITCHER	
1st 6-3	4th HR	6th W/		Steve Trachsel
8th W/				CUBS STARTER, 5⅔ IP

COUNT	ON BASE	OUTS
0/0	0	2

SOSA	PACE	GRIFFEY
58	70	50

FINAL: Cardinals 6, Cubs 3

Cardinals' record: 71-73

341 ft.

The record-breaker, McGwire's shortest home run of the season, barely cleared the left field wall and landed in an open area under the stands.

record-breaking moment as a wave of jubilation cascaded through the stadium, the streets of St. Louis, the country and points beyond.

McGwire's history-making moment came in the fourth inning on the first pitch he saw from Chicago righthander Steve Trachsel. The bases-empty blow lifted him onto a single-season plateau that hadn't been ascended in baseball history, and it came in his 145th game, nine fewer than Babe Ruth needed to hit 60 in 1927 and a whopping 18 fewer than Roger Maris needed to hit 61 in 1961.

It also came in a Cardinals victory over the hated Cubs, with Sammy Sosa, Mac's chief challenger with 58 homers, watching from his right field position. The record-breaker was McGwire's 50th off righthanded pitching and only his 19th of less than 400 feet.

■ "What a perfect way to end the homestand, by hitting 62 for the city of St. Louis and all the fans. I truly wanted to do it here, and I did. Thank you, St. Louis." —*McGwire*

■ "It's just a home run. We lost the ballgame. That's what is most disappointing. ... I'm hoping they'll be talking about Steve Trachsel (years from now) helping the Cubs get to the World Series. I hope that's what they will be talking about." —*Cubs pitcher Steve Trachsel, McGwire victim No. 62*

■ "I jumped and yelled and screamed like everybody else. It brings back the little kid in you. We're teammates, but we're fans, too. It brings back the great emotions of playing baseball as a kid, the positive things about the game that have been overshadowed." —*Cardinals infielder Pat Kelly*

"Swing and a shot into the corner. It might make it! There it is: 62, folks! It just got over the left field wall in the corner. And we have a new home run champion! A new Sultan of Swat! It's Mark McGwire! He touches them all. Unbelievable."

—The historic call of homer 62 by Cardinals radio broadcaster Mike Shannon

PARTY OF ONE: *One of the few unhappy faces at Busch Stadium September 8 belonged to Cubs righthander Steve Trachsel (above), who fumed as Big Mac (in the background) danced around the bases after his record-breaking 62nd homer. The blow over the left field wall (above left) brought both tears and cheers (right page, below) from the older and younger Cardinals faithful.*

Homer 62 Quick Facts

- 50th off righthanded pitching
- 19th of less than 400 feet
- 32nd at Busch Stadium
- 15th on a Tuesday
- 11th in the fourth inning

- 30th with the bases empty
- 9th on the first pitch
- 46th in night games
- 7th against the Cubs
- 25th since the All-Star Game
- 145th game of the season
- 1st time a non-Yankee has held the record since 1919
- 341 feet, McGwire's shortest of the season

HAVING A BALL: *Not lost in the excitement of a magical moment was home run ball No. 62, which was returned to McGwire by Tim Forneris (right), a member of the Busch Stadium grounds crew, during a postgame ceremony that honored baseball's new home run king. Mac's father, John McGwire (second from right), commissioner Bud Selig (left) and broadcaster Jack Buck (second from left) were center stage for the festivities.*

"Unbelievable ... class"

For 11 glorious minutes on the night of September 8, the baseball world stood still. Or, more accurately, Mark McGwire held it motionless in the palms of his powerful hands.

As the new home run king, the first heir to the throne

in 37 years, Big Mac wielded that kind of power. His magic wand had driven away all the negative remnants and hard feelings left over from the 1994 baseball strike and his sense of drama and accommodating personality had returned the game to its feel-good past. Now it was time to enjoy the fruits of his labor.

"I dedicate this home run to the whole city of St. Louis and all the fans here," McGwire said into a microphone that carried his words to a packed house at Busch Stadium. "Thanks for all your support. It's unbelievable. All my family, everybody. Chicago Cubs. Sammy Sosa. Unbelievable ... class."

The words triggered another in a long line of roars from fans, players, officials and any other living being that had found an empty nook in a Busch Stadium

RECORD HUGS: *An emotional McGwire delivered home-run hugs to his parents (above) and former wife Kathy Williamson (left) after trotting into uncharted territory.*

cranny. Among those paying tribute were such Cardinals of yesteryear as Stan Musial, Lou Brock, Red Schoendienst and Ozzie Smith.

"I think this is the biggest thrill I've ever had in baseball," said Hall of Fame broadcaster Jack Buck, the Cardinals' radio voice for 44 years. "This was the most monumental home run in the history of the game. I don't think anything that's ever happened in this ballpark compares to what we've just observed."

The most anticipated home run since Hank Aaron hit No. 715 in 1974 was only the start of McGwire's victory parade. After "a sweet, sweet run around the bases," McGwire picked up his 10-year-old son Matthew near home plate, gave him a bear hug and planted a big kiss that seemed to punctuate the moment. Then he was mobbed by Cardinals teammates and congratulated by Chicago rival Sammy Sosa, who joined the celebration from his right field position to exchange bashes and hugs with the enemy.

NICE RIDE: *Roger Maris' children (top photo) inspect the bat their father used to set his homer mark in 1961. The ultimate victory laps were taken in Mac's Cardinal-red '62 Corvette, a gift from the team.*

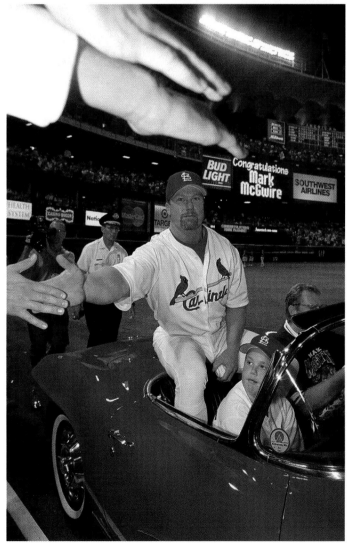

After blowing more kisses into the stands and saluting his parents, McGwire jogged triumphantly over to the first-base box seats in a gesture that would cement his status as a genuine American hero. He stepped over the railing and shared his moment with the children of Roger Maris, hugging them and giving them the respect their father had never received during the 1961 season in which he surpassed Babe Ruth's 34-year-old single-season homer record.

"My body's still numb. I'm extremely happy for Mark. For all he's done for baseball. ...I couldn't be happier," said Roger Jr. "For Mark to be the person he is and to mean what he means to baseball and to the fans of America, I couldn't think of a better person to be the new home run king for a single season.

"I think Dad would be happy for Mark and proud of

SUMMER OF 62: *McGwire's record-breaking home run triggered celebrations all over St. Louis and triggered a clamor for copies of a St. Louis Post-Dispatch extra (left), which was printed and being sold before the September 8 game had even ended.*

MASS CONFUSION: *McGwire, who has never been far from the maddening crowd, saw the relentless media (below) and expectant fans (right) swell to record proportions in anticipation of a record night at Busch Stadium.*

him for his accomplishments. He would've been very proud of Mark as a player, but I think more so as a person."

Earlier in the day, Mac had made another Maris connection—with Roger's bat, which was brought from Cooperstown as a Hall of Fame gesture for the moment that was about to unfold.

"I touched it," McGwire said. "I touched it with my heart. Now I can honestly say my bat's going right next to his and I'm damn proud of it.

"Thanks to Babe, Roger and everybody who's watching up there."

The rest of the game, played amid a

steady roar, merely set the stage for postgame festivities that included McGwire's triumphant trip around Busch Stadium in a 1962 Cardinal-red Corvette convertible—the team's gift to the new home run champion—and a memorable tribute from commissioner Bud Selig that labeled it "one of the most historic nights in baseball history" and St. Louis as "the crown jewel of baseball franchises."

But National League president Leonard Coleman might have put the home run into more accurate perspective.

"The shot heard 'round the world was Bobby Thomson's home run in 1951 to win the pennant for the New York Giants," Coleman said. "This was the shot seen 'round the world."

PLAY IT AGAIN, SAM: *Sharing the 62 moment with McGwire was Cubs right fielder Sammy Sosa, who had more than a passing interest.*

THE DAY AFTER: *McGwire's 62nd home run was not taken lightly by St. Louis fans, who celebrated the feat with a downtown party the next day. Among the party hearty congregation were 3-year-old Brittney Dunworth (above middle, right) and 5-year-old sister Taylor.*

The Race

Sosa's

Weekend

"I have to admit, I was one of them," said Cubs teammate Mark Grace, who ended the Sunday game with a 10th-inning home run—while Sosa waited in the on-deck circle. "It was chilling when McGwire did it. I was dumbfounded. That put him four ahead and I pretty much thought the home run race was over.

"But when my friend Sammy gets hot, he gets them in a hurry. And right now, he's hot."

Sosa's Sunday effort highlighted a wild, emotional day at Wrigley Field. It started with a record crowd of 40,846 hoping for a Sosa home run and a victory that would inch the Cubs closer to a post-season berth and it ended with jubilant Chicago players carrying Sosa around the field on their shoulders. The fans got everything they wanted—and then some. The moment was not lost on the man who would be king.

"For the first time, I'm so emotional," a choked-up Sosa said after the Sunday game. "When I got to 62, I have to say it was something unbelievable, something I can't believe what I'm doing. I said to Mark McGwire, 'Wait for me.' Now we're together."

The Cubs were trailing 6-3 in the fifth inning when Sosa rocketed a Bronswell Patrick changeup onto Waveland Avenue, triggering a wild scramble by souvenir-seeking fans who had gathered with hopes of catching homer No. 61. "It was just an unbelievable feeling, an emotional moment for me," said Sosa, who was embraced by Grace after his stutter-stepping home run trot and over-whelmed by a roaring crowd that demanded the customary curtain call.

DON'T LOOK BACK: *The hot breath McGwire felt on the back of his neck September 13 belonged to Sosa, who assaulted the Brewers and claimed a share of the single-season home run record.*

Down but not out after watching McGwire hit his record-breaking 62nd home run in a September 8 game at St. Louis, Chicago's Sammy Sosa drilled four homers in a three-game weekend series against Milwaukee and set the stage for the most dramatic home run race in baseball history.

Sosa connected for homer No. 59 in a 13-11 Friday night loss to the Brewers and joined McGwire, Ruth and Roger Maris in the exclusive 60-something club the next day as the Cubs rallied for a 15-12 victory. But the best was yet to come. Sosa delivered a pair of 480-foot lightning bolts in a wild 11-10 Sunday victory that shot him past Maris' previous record of 61 and tied McGwire's all-time mark of 62.

But the real celebration was triggered by a ninth-inning solo blast off Eric Plunk that sailed onto Waveland Avenue and cut the Chicago deficit to 10-9. Only two curtain calls would appease the crowd and the game had to be delayed so ushers could gather up debris thrown onto the field. The inspired Cubs rallied to force extra innings and set up Grace's 10th-inning heroics.

"That was the greatest series of baseball I've ever been involved in," Grace said. "I'll remember this series until my deathbed. I'm just sorry that I hit the home run and that Sammy didn't get to come up and do it himself. I know that's what the fans wanted to see."

The three-day, four-homer blitz gave Sosa 10 home runs off the Milwaukee pitching staff and ended his five-game homerless drought.

63

"A home run is an earned run and that upsets me any time. ... It really doesn't matter if it's a guy's first homer or his 100th."

—Pirates pitcher Jason Christiansen

It was a cameo appearance, a gift at-bat for the Busch Stadium faithful who had not expected to see McGwire in the opener of a doubleheader against the Pittsburgh Pirates. But, like he had done so many times in a movie-like season, Big Mac attached a memory to the moment.

"It was just a moment," Cardinals manager Tony La Russa said after watching McGwire deliver his 63rd home run in an unusual pinch-hit role. "How do you do that? You've seen it. He's been doing that for a year and two months. People cheer him, 'C'mon Mark, we want you to hit one.' Boom. He hits it."

McGwire's 450th career homer, a towering 385-foot drive into the left-center field

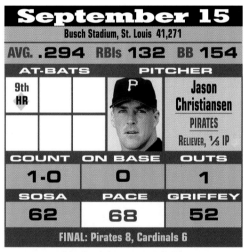

September 15
Busch Stadium, St. Louis 41,271

AVG. **.294** RBIs **132** BB **154**

AT-BATS	PITCHER
9th HR	**Jason Christiansen** PIRATES Reliever, ⅓ IP

COUNT	ON BASE	OUTS
1-0	**0**	**1**

SOSA	PACE	GRIFFEY
62	**68**	**52**

FINAL: Pirates 8, Cardinals 6

Cardinals' record: 74-77

385 ft.

McGwire's first pinch-hit homer of the season landed in the left-center field bleachers at Busch Stadium.

bleachers, came on a 1-0 pitch from Pirates lefthander Jason Christiansen and allowed him to reclaim the single-season home run record from Sammy Sosa, who had caught Big Mac at 62. McGwire, who had been battling minor back spasms, batted in the ninth inning with the bases empty and the Cardinals trailing by three runs, a situation that normally would not pry him from the bench.

"Under ordinary circumstances, you wouldn't send McGwire up in that situation," Pirates manager Gene Lamont said. "But I understood why Tony did it. It was a good idea."

McGwire played the second game of the doubleheader, a 9-3 St. Louis victory, and collected a double and two walks. His first-game homer, which came one week after his festive 62nd record-breaker, overshadowed the two-homer effort of Cardinals rookie J.D. Drew.

SOSA'S 63rd *One day after McGwire had hit his record 63rd homer, Sammy Sosa pulled back into a tie with a game-deciding grand slam in the eighth inning of a 6-3 victory at San Diego.*

Sosa's dramatic 434-foot drive off Brian Boehringer landed in the upper deck and snapped a 2-2 tie. He had doubled home the Cubs' first two runs and drove in all six runs in the game. The win gave Chicago a half-game lead over the New York Mets in the race for the N.L. wild-card berth.

"I never thought I would get No. 63 with the bases loaded," Sosa said.

■ "Whatever I end up with, I end up with. I've done what I've done. Does it make it any less if I don't lead? No. Because what I've done and what Sammy has done is fantastic." —*McGwire*

64

"Never forget how amazing this man is. I keep searching for a way to describe it."

—Cardinals manager Tony La Russa

Turnabout is fair play. Sammy Sosa used a four-homer weekend blitz against Milwaukee to spring back into baseball's Great Home Run Race, so it seemed only fitting McGwire should break a tie at 63 and reclaim the single-season record in the opener of a three-game series against the Brewers.

McGwire regained his one-homer edge with a 417-foot fourth-inning shot over the left-center field fence at County Stadium and then barely missed two more with towering upper-deck drives that hooked foul in the sixth and eighth innings. The message was clear: Mac's post-62 lull was over and his home run battery was recharged.

"He put three great swings on the ball," said manager Tony La Russa after watching his team win its third straight game and reach the .500 mark for the first time since June 24. "That last one was really, really close."

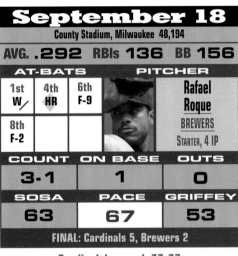

September 18

County Stadium, Milwaukee 48,194

AVG. **.292** RBIs **136** BB **156**

AT-BATS			PITCHER
1st W/	4th HR	6th F-9	Rafael Roque
8th F-2			BREWERS STARTER, 4 IP

COUNT	ON BASE	OUTS
3-1	1	0

SOSA	PACE	GRIFFEY
63	67	53

FINAL: Cardinals 5, Brewers 2

Cardinals' record: 77-77

The ball sailed over the left-center field fence and down a runway at Milwaukee's County Stadium.

McGwire's 64th homer came in the Cardinals' 154th game—the schedule Babe Ruth played in 1927 when he hit 60 for the Yankees. It was his second home run in 24 at-bats since hitting record-breaking 62.

"There's such a buildup to what I did—and you do it. I basically didn't know where I was for a couple of days," McGwire said. "I think that's explainable."

McGwire's record-breaker came against rookie Rafael Roque and a staff that had surrendered 10 home runs to Sosa.

SOSA *The Chicago Cubs dropped a tough-to-swallow 6-4 decision to Cincinnati on September 18 and Sammy Sosa completed his second straight game without a home run, falling one behind McGwire in the Great Race.*

"I have to say they pitch me real carefully," said Sosa, who was 0-for-4 and failed to get a ball out of the infield against Reds pitchers. "They didn't give me much to hit today."

Despite the loss, the Cubs remained a game ahead of the New York Mets in their pursuit of the N.L. wild-card berth. The Mets lost to Florida.

■ "There's nothing better than playing a baseball game in front of a full house. I know for quite some time now that a lot of fans across America have come specifically to watch me. At first, it was very overwhelming, but I got used to it. ... You don't come to a baseball game to watch one guy. But I've learned to accept it." *—McGwire*

65

"I couldn't care less if he hits 150 home runs. As an umpire, you can't get caught up in that."

—Umpire Bob Davidson, after ruling McGwire's potential 66th home run a double

No. 65 was a gift for Matthew. No. 65A was a little spice for the previously controversy-free great home run celebration of 1998.

"I asked him how many home runs he wanted his dad to hit," said McGwire, referring to a conversation he had with 10-year-old son Matt just before leaving for spring training. "He looked me in the eye and said, 'Sixty-five.'"

No problem. Big Mac filled Matt's order in the first inning of an easy win at Milwaukee's County Stadium when he drilled a Scott Karl pitch 423 feet into the left field seats, raising the single-season home run bar to 65—two ahead of Chicago's Sammy Sosa. The home run, which lifted

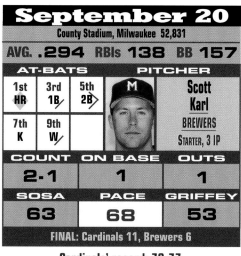

September 20

County Stadium, Milwaukee 52,831

AVG. .294   RBIs 138   BB 157

AT-BATS

1st HR	3rd 1B	5th 2B
7th K	9th W	

PITCHER

Scott Karl
BREWERS
STARTER, 3 IP

COUNT	ON BASE	OUTS
2-1	1	1

SOSA	PACE	GRIFFEY
63	68	53

FINAL: Cardinals 11, Brewers 6

Cardinals' record: 79-77

No. 65 sailed high into the left field seats at Milwaukee's County Stadium.

McGwire's career total to 452 and tied him with Carl Yastrzemski for 20th place on the all-time list, was one of five struck by the Cardinals.

"Sixty-five had a big meaning because that's the number my son set before spring training, so it means a lot to me," McGwire said. "That's all I thought about when I was running around the bases."

The two-run blow was just an appetizer. In the fifth inning, McGwire drove a pitch from Rod Henderson toward the seats in left-center. The ball appeared to clear the yellow bar atop the outfield wall, but umpire Bob Davidson stopped McGwire at second base, ruling a fan had reached over the fence and interfered with its flight. The crowd roared its disapproval, but McGwire had to be satisfied with his ground-rule double and still-uncomfortable home run lead over Sosa.

SOSA *On Sammy Sosa Day at Chicago's Wrigley Field, Cubs fans saluted their Dominican star and threw a festive pregame party in his honor. But an 0-for-5 day by Sosa and a 7-3 Chicago loss to Cincinnati threw a damper on the occasion.*

Adding to everybody's discomfort was news McGwire had homered again in Milwaukee, increasing his lead over Sosa to 65-63.

Sosa, who saw his hitless streak reach 17 at-bats, failed to get a ball out of the infield for a third straight game.

■ "You're not supposed to hit 65 homers. We know how important Matthew is to him, but you can't just hit 65 homers because your son asks you to. But here we are with six games left and he has 65. It's unbelievable. Sixty-five?" —*Cardinals catcher Tom Lampkin*

Television replays and fan testimonials disputed Davidson's judgment. It appeared the only "leaning" that took place was over an inside fence, thanks to the crush of ball-seekers pushing from behind.

"It was definitely a home run," said Allan Riesbeck, a partially paralyzed Iowa man who got a hand on the ball but couldn't hold it. "I was careful not to get my hands over the field. It was a home run. I went numb when they gave him a double."

Michael Chapes, who caught the ball but had it snatched out of his glove, was even more numb, thanks to the escort he received out of the park and a $518 fine he got for interfering with a ball in play. "It was definitely a home run. This whole thing makes me sick," he said.

Although the fans roared their disapproval, the Cardinals did not put up much of an argument at the time. But the team appealed to the National League after the game—an appeal that was denied the next day. The Cardinals argued that their victory over the Brewers was lopsided and McGwire scored anyway on Brian Jordan's single.

"After further review, it looked like a home run. The replay shows it. I didn't see the ball come back in play," said McGwire, who had to settle for a 65-63 home run advantage over Sammy Sosa entering the final week of the season. "(Davidson) said (the fan) came over the fence. I didn't see it running, but when I saw it on videotape, the man who caught the ball never came over the yellow line."

DOUBLE TALK: *Fans battle for potential homer No. 66 as Brewers center fielder Marquis Grissom looks for the ball. Umpire Bob Davidson ruled fan interference and stopped McGwire at second.*

The ball screamed toward the left-center field seats as more than 50,000 sets of eyes strained to see its final destination. Home run No. 66 would be icing on the cake for the near-capacity Milwaukee County Stadium crowd that already had witnessed No. 65 in the ever-growing legacy of Mac moments.

The ball disappeared, touching off a mighty roar and the now-familiar melding of bodies in search of the ultimate souvenir. But as McGwire rounded second base, he was suddenly halted in mid-home run trot by umpire Bob Davidson, who delivered some startling news. Route 66 would end at second—a ground-rule double instead of a home run—because a fan had reached over the yellow-topped outfield fence and interfered with a ball that would not have reached the seats.

"The ball got out there in about half a second," Davidson explained after the game. "When I saw it, the fan was leaning over and the ball hit him below the yellow line. I saw the ball good. To me, the fan was over."

STOP SIGN: *Mac lost home run 66 when umpire Bob Davidson ruled that overzealous fans had given his ball an illegal lift into the stands.*

Ready for the Grand Finale

Two down, four games to play. No problem, at least not for Cubs right fielder Sammy Sosa in the magic Summer of '98.

The unshakable Sosa, hitless in his last 21 at-bats and seemingly on the verge of being closed out in the Great Home Run Chase, climbed out of his funk and delivered a 1-2 punch that set up a dramatic finale to one of the greatest chapters in baseball history. Sosa hit homers 64 and 65 in consecutive innings of a game at Milwaukee, drawing even with McGwire in the race for baseball's most exalted single-season record.

"This is my lucky team," said a smiling Sosa after hitting his 11th and 12th homers of the season against the Brewers. "Whatever has happened with the Brewers, how can you explain? I have to say I was strong. I came back today and felt great today."

Sosa ended his five-day struggle with style. Home run 64 came in the fifth off left-hander Rafael Roque, the same pitcher who had allowed McGwire's 64th. The opposite-field solo shot was followed by a bases-empty drive over the center field fence in the sixth off Rod Henderson, the pitcher who had surrendered McGwire's disallowed 66th homer.

"On the second, (Henderson) threw me a lot of breaking pitches," Sosa said. "I was fighting for that at-bat. He got two strikes, I relaxed, waited to see a good pitch and then he threw me a fastball."

Sosa's homers helped the playoff-hungry Cubs build a 7-0 lead, but Milwaukee fought back and handed Chicago a devastating defeat when left fielder Brant Brown dropped a two-out, bases-loaded fly ball that allowed three runs to score in the ninth inning. The shocking conclusion put a damper on Sosa's heroics.

"If I finish first or if I finish last (in home runs), it is no different," Sosa said. "I have another thing to do. It is the playoffs."

SOMETHING'S BREWING: *Sosa's unyielding challenge to McGwire stirred patriotic emotions, both at home in the Dominican Republic and among the Dominican flag-waving fans he encountered at every National League stop.*

The Final Weekend

66

"One thing about this game is that you don't usually get to choose your fame."

—Espos pitcher Shayne Bennett, who gave up homer 66

After a week filled with disallowed home runs, foul homers and drives to the warning track, McGwire finally broke through against the Montreal Expos—and his 375-foot shot into Busch Stadium's left field seats came just in the nick of time.

No. 66, unlike the four that preceded it, was not a major league record because 45 minutes earlier Sammy Sosa had connected for his 66th home run in a game at Houston. It was the first time Sosa had beaten him to a record milestone and the long-distance duel was waged in the third-to-last games for both McGwire's Cardinals and Sosa's Cubs.

"It was pretty obvious, of course. How could you not? The crowd said something," said McGwire when asked if he knew Sosa had jumped ahead in the home run chase. "But then again, like I've said 1,000 times, it really doesn't matter.

September 25

Busch Stadium, St. Louis 48,159

AVG. .293	RBIs 140	BB 161

AT-BATS			PITCHER	
1st W∕	3rd F-7	5th HR		Shayne Bennett
7th 1B∕	9th K			EXPOS
				RELIEVER, ⅔ IP

COUNT	ON BASE	OUTS
1-2	1	2

SOSA	PACE	GRIFFEY
66	67	56

FINAL: Cardinals 6, Expos 5

Cardinals' record: 82-78

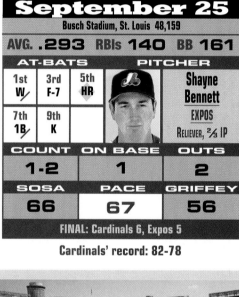

McGwire's record-tying 66th homer landed in the left field seats at Busch Stadium.

He controls his destiny, and I control my destiny."

Big Mac's fifth-inning at-bat against Shayne Bennett appeared to be destined for more of the frustration that had been coming in steady doses. He jumped on Bennett's first pitch and sent a towering drive toward the left field corner, but the ball settled into the upper deck, inches foul.

"It was foul, but it wasn't foul far," umpire Joe West said. "I think (it) went over the pole."

Four pitches later, McGwire ended his three-game homerless skid and keyed a victory that also featured a pair of homers by rookie J.D. Drew.

SOSA *Homer 66 temporarily lifted Sosa past McGwire, but it couldn't lift his Cubs to a much-needed victory over Houston. The Cubs, trying to keep pace in the race for the N.L. wild-card spot, lost to the Astros, 6-2, and finished the day in a three-way tie with the New York Mets and San Francisco.*

Sosa's fourth-inning blast, which gave him the distinction of reaching the 66 plateau before McGwire, tied the game 2-2, but that's all the scoring the Cubs could manage. The Mets dropped a 6-5 decision to Atlanta and the Giants defeated the Rockies, 8-6, to force the tie with two games remaining.

■ "I am going to have fun. I'm going to do my best at whatever I can do. I'm not going away hanging my head at all. If (Sosa's) up by one or we're tied or whatever may happen, it's going to be an exciting weekend." —*McGwire, looking ahead to the season's final two games.*

The leader—for less than an hour

August 19. Chicago's Wrigley Field. Sammy Sosa vs. Mark McGwire in baseball's 1998 production of Home Run Derby. Sosa blasts a fifth-inning homer off St. Louis' Kent Bottenfield and passes McGwire for the first time all season. But the lead lasts only 58 minutes as Big Mac responds with his tying 48th home run in the eighth and a game-winning 49th homer in the 10th.

September 25. The final weekend at St. Louis' Busch Stadium and Houston's Astrodome, 750 miles apart. Sosa pounds a pitch from Astros righthander Jose Lima 462 feet for his major league-record 66th home run, breaking a 2-day-old tie with McGwire. But this lead lasts only 45 minutes as Big Mac responds with a fifth-inning, 375-foot blast off Montreal righthander Shayne Bennett.

"A classic. It's like *Gone With the Wind*," said Cardinals outfielder John Mabry. "It's an amazing thing to look up and see the flash that Sammy just hit 66, and then Mac hits one, too. You wouldn't believe it unless you were here to see it. It's like one of those bad baseball movies that people make."

But great theater in baseball's season of hope. It marked the 21st time Sosa and McGwire had homered on the same day and the fourth time they had been tied (at 62, 63, 65 and 66) since Big Mac broke Roger Maris' single-season home run record. Turnabout was

fair play for No. 66. After being stalked relentlessly through the second half of the season by Sosa, it seemed only fair that McGwire should return the favor.

"He's been doing things like that since opening day," Cardinals manager Tony La Russa said of his big first baseman. "When has Mark done anything that's anywhere near normal and natural?"

While that flair for the dramatic kept fans and teammates on the edge of the seats, McGwire and Sosa remained true to their emotions.

"My feeling is that what (Sosa) and I have done, nobody should be disappointed," McGwire said. "We're two guys who have done something that's never been done in the history of the game."

Sosa agreed. "I'm not here to chase anybody, just to do my job," he said. "I felt great when I hit mine and then when Mark McGwire hit No. 66, too."

McGwire even went so far as to suggest that a home run tie might be the perfect ending. But not everybody shared that sentiment.

"As far as I'm concerned—I'm not speaking for the ownership or the coaches or the front office—Mark McGwire's home run record is the most important thing the next two days," said La Russa. "That sounds like heresy for me to say it. But he deserves everything we've got behind him. We're pulling for him real, real hard. We're probably more excited than he is."

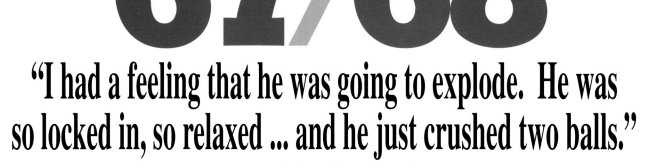

67/68

"I had a feeling that he was going to explode. He was so locked in, so relaxed ... and he just crushed two balls."

——Cardinals catcher Tom Lampkin

With two more swings, McGwire cut an 838-foot swath in the 1998 home run race and staked yet another claim as the greatest single-season home run hitter in history.

While Sammy Sosa was going 2-for-4 without a homer at Houston, Big Mac muscled up twice against Montreal and broke the home run record for the fifth and sixth times.

"Does it look like he's under pressure? He hit two today," marveled catcher Tom Lampkin when asked about McGwire's state of mind entering the season's final day. "The mental aspect of his game is amazing. Nobody knows what he's going through because no one has hit 68 home runs before. I can't even fathom what goes through that guy's mind."

After he'd struck out against Expos starter Dustin Hermanson in his first at-bat, Big Mac hit

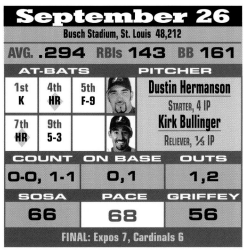

September 26
Busch Stadium, St. Louis 48,212

AVG. .294	RBIs 143	BB 161

AT-BATS			PITCHER
1st K	4th HR	5th F-9	**Dustin Hermanson** STARTER, 4 IP
7th HR	9th 5-3		**Kirk Bullinger** RELIEVER, ⅓ IP

COUNT	ON BASE	OUTS
0-0, 1-1	0, 1	1, 2

SOSA	PACE	GRIFFEY
66	68	56

FINAL: Expos 7, Cardinals 6

Cardinals' record: 82-79

Home run 67 sailed into the left field seats and No. 68 prompted a souvenir scramble in the left center field bleachers.

Hermanson's first pitch of the fourth inning 403 feet to left field. He pumped his fist into the air on his way to first, and was congratulated by Expos third baseman Shane Andrews on his way home.

In the seventh, McGwire drilled a low sinker from Kirk Bullinger 435 feet to left-center, marking his ninth multihomer game of 1998 and giving him a 2-stroke lead over Sosa. As he approached first, McGwire found himself still holding the bat, high in the air to celebrate the moment—like an artist who'd supplied the final stroke to a canvas.

The Expos, however, pushed across a ninth-inning run and escaped with a victory. But not before retiring McGwire on a grounder to third for the last out of the game. After which, he received yet another standing ovation.

SOSA *Neither of Sosa's hits were homers, but he was instrumental in a 3-2 Cubs victory over Houston that kept them tied with San Francisco for the N.L. wild-card playoff position entering the season's final day.*

Sosa's one-out single in the eighth inning set up a two-run Cubs rally that broke a 1-1 tie and gave them their second victory in seven games. That was good enough for Sammy on a day when Big Mac was having deep thoughts. "I've always said that I'm more interested in the wild card. ... However it finishes, it's been a great year," Sosa said.

■ "I completely forgot the bat was still in my hand. I said, 'I've got to get rid of this thing.'" —*McGwire, on his bat-raising home run trot after homer 68*

■ "It's not the physical grind; it's the mental grind. ... I've never used my mind any more than this year." —*McGwire*

GOING, GOING, GONE: *The eyes have it as flight 68 is monitored by McGwire, Expos pitcher Kirk Bullinger and the thousands of fans on hand for another historic day at St. Louis' Busch Stadium.*

SAD ENDING: *Home run No. 67 was served up to McGwire (far left) by Montreal righthander Dustin Hermanson, who contemplated the error of his ways shortly thereafter in the Expos' dugout.*

69/70

"If Mac wrote this script, then he'll get more nominations than *Titanic*."

——*Cardinals outfielder John Mabry*

Like a great actor taking his final bow, McGwire closed the most sensational single-season home run performance in major league history by lifting his record into a new dimension.

McGwire, who had been locked in a neck-and-neck home run race with Sammy Sosa with two games to play, turned the season's final weekend into a riveting and joyous victory trot at St. Louis' Busch Stadium.

With Mac-crazed fans roaring their approval, he slammed homers 69 and 70 on the final day of the season to bring his weekend total to five in three games and finish four ahead of the defeated but still amazing Sosa.

"To say the least, I'm amazed," McGwire said. "Hitting 70, I've never thought about it or dreamt about it. ... I'm speechless, really. I can't

believe I did it. Can you? It blows me away."

Relaxed and zoned in after trailing Sosa for 45 minutes only two days earlier, McGwire smashed a breaking pitch from Montreal's Mike Thurman into the left field seats in the third inning for No. 69.

And he completed his second straight multihomer game in the seventh with a line drive off Carl Pavano—a three-run shot that broke a 3-3 tie. After what would prove to be the game-winning homer, McGwire was congratulated by Montreal catcher Mike Barrett and the entire Expos infield.

McGwire also singled to raise his final average to .299. "That (.300) is something nobody's really talked about— I've hit a lot of home runs but I've maintained an average," McGwire said. "And I'm proud of it."

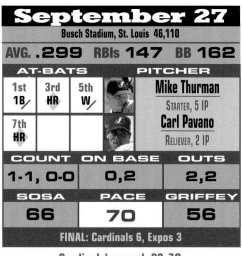

September 27
Busch Stadium, St. Louis 46,110

AVG. .299	RBIs 147	BB 162

AT-BATS			PITCHER
1st 1B	3rd HR	5th W	**Mike Thurman** STARTER, 5 IP
7th HR			**Carl Pavano** RELIEVER, 2 IP

COUNT	ON BASE	OUTS
1-1, 0-0	0,2	2,2

SOSA	PACE	GRIFFEY
66	70	56

FINAL: Cardinals 6, Expos 3

Cardinals' record: 83-79

377 ft.
370 ft.

McGwire's towering 69th homer landed in the left field seats; historic No. 70 was a line drive into a party room just above the left field fence.

SOSA *While McGwire was distancing himself from Sosa in the home run chase, Sammy was enjoying the satisfaction of helping his team claim a wild-card playoff berth.*

Sosa, who was homerless over his final three games, went 2-for-5 and drove in his major league-leading 158th run in an 11-inning, 4-3 final-day loss to Houston. Then he was 2-for-4 (two singles) in Chicago's 5-3 victory over San Francisco in the one-game playoff for the N.L. wild-card berth. Sosa finished with a .308 average.

■ "I'm like in awe of myself right now." —*McGwire*

■ "He's a massive human being. He's a big dude ... and he hit a good pitch. I didn't lay it in there. I was going after him. He went right after me and hit a home run. I guess he won." —*No. 70 victim Carl Pavano*

"Swing and it's ... get up, baby! Get up, get up, get up.
HOME RUN. He's done it again!
Seventy home runs. Take a ride on that for history! ... How can
you end a season better than Mark McGwire has just done?"

—*The historic call of homer 70 by Cardinals broadcaster Mike Shannon*

'Stranger than fiction'

It started with a distant thud and ended with fireworks. In between, the final weekend of the 1998 season was filled with enough drama, excitement, amazement and emotional thunder to overwhelm even the most hardened and grizzled of baseball fans.

The thud was provided by Sammy Sosa when he drove a Jose Lima pitch into the fourth deck of Houston's Astrodome and startled the St. Louis fans who had gathered at Busch Stadium to watch McGwire complete the final leg of his record home run journey. The fireworks started 45 minutes later when Big Mac answered with his 66th home run, reclaiming a share of the major league record he had held for almost three weeks.

| 25 MC GWIRE | 70 |
| 21 SOSA | 66 |

UNCHARTED TERRITORY: *The scoreboard homer count (left page, below) seemed like something right out of a fairy tale when McGwire hit No. 70 and enjoyed a dugout celebration with coach Dave Parker (right, left photo) and teammates. On the at-bat before his history-making blow, Mac had dipped and dodged away from Mike Thurman pitches (photos below) while drawing his 162nd walk.*

"I just think he's been incredible all year long. And somehow the next three days he's going to do whatever he has to do—some way, somehow," Cardinals manager Tony La Russa had predicted before the Friday night game against Montreal.

Having taken and answered Sosa's best punch, a suddenly relaxed McGwire drove La Russa's crystal ball into the outer reaches of everybody's wildest dreams. First he took the lead with home runs 67 and 68 in a memorable Saturday afternoon game against the Expos.

68!

"He came into the dugout after he hit his (66th) home run, and he looked at me and just exhaled," said Cardinals catcher Tom Lampkin, one of McGwire's closest friends. "It was like he just had the biggest weight lifted off his shoulder. He didn't say anything, but it was like he finally got over the hump. He tied Sammy again.

"And I came in (Saturday), and I never had as good a feeling as I did about him hitting two home runs. Because after he gave me that little sign on the bench, I had a feeling that he was going to explode. He was so locked in, so relaxed, as if he had no pressure on him at all. And he just crushed two balls."

The first, a fourth-inning shot off Expos ace Dustin Hermanson, traveled 403 feet and prompted a

MASTERPIECE THEATER:
Home run No. 68 was worthy of a special bat-tossing gesture (right) on Saturday. Homer 69, which was saluted by first base coach Dave McKay (below left), was merely a Sunday appetizer for the grand finale Mac would deliver a few innings later. A special 69 salute was delivered by Kerry Woodson Jr. (white shirt, bottom photo), the St. Louis fan who caught the ball.

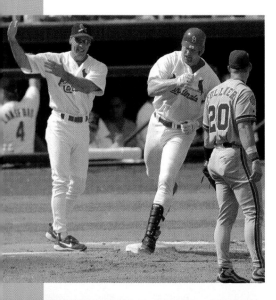

"I'll never let this season go," McGwire said during

fist-pumping trot reminiscent of his 60th, 61st and 62nd homers. The second, a 435-footer off Kirk Bullinger in the seventh inning, was watched by McGwire as he trotted down the first-base line, bat extended in the air like a magic wand, and he was escorted around the bases by another wave of cheers from the roaring crowd.

Then, before the Saturday excitement could even reach a level pitch, McGwire punctuated his big finish with another two-homer barrage—69 and 70—in a Sunday afternoon party at Busch Stadium.

70!

"It's one of the most special things we'll ever see in our lives," said Drew Baur, one of the Cardinals' owners.

"I'm speechless, really," McGwire said. "I can't believe I did it."

The impact of the moment, the creation of a new monument in baseball's record book, was not lost on Cardinals outfielder John Mabry.

"This is something you can tell your kids you were a part of," Mabry said. "You can't say enough about it, what it's meant to the game and the people who have been around it. He's not only in the hearts of St. Louis, but he's in the hearts of the country and even around the world."

It seemed only fitting that Big Mac would break ground on his own lofty plateau on his final swing of the incredible season with a three-run, game-winning blow. Homer 69 had sent the Busch Stadium crowd into another tizzy, complete with two curtain calls. But No. 70—a vicious line drive to left that shot out of the park in a blink of the eye—generated a whole new feeling of euphoria from a crowd and a city that should have been running low on emotional energy.

The 70 celebration, while lacking the electricity generated by 62, was more like a sustained canonization of a baseball god. McGwire tipped his cap, saluted, smiled and waved to the St. Louis faithful

the final series. "It might never happen again."

In perspective...

Quick facts to contemplate while trying to digest McGwire's 70-home run season:

■ McGwire reached his amazing milestone on 509 official at-bats, 31 fewer than Babe Ruth needed to hit 60 homers in 1927 and 81 fewer than Roger Maris needed to raise the single-season record bar to 61 in 1961.

■ McGwire has averaged 60 home runs over the last three seasons and his three-year total of 180 is 19 more than Ruth's best three-year run. It is, in fact, better than Ruth's best non-consecutive three years (173).

■ McGwire didn't play favorites, hitting home runs off 65 different pitchers. The only repeat victims were Arizona's Jeff Suppan, Philadelphia's Tyler Green, New York's Rick Reed, Colorado's John Thomson and Florida's Livan Hernandez.

■ McGwire finished the season with nine more home runs than singles.

■ Mac's homer total was three better than Earl Webb's 1931 record for doubles in a season.

■ The 70-homer total was three higher than the Cardinals team hit in 1982 en route to a World Series championship.

■ McGwire hit 38 home runs at Busch Stadium. Only three Cardinals in history (Johnny Mize, Rogers Hornsby and Stan Musial) have hit that many in a single season—home and away.

■ McGwire hit a major league record-tying 32 home runs on the road. Only seven Cardinals (Mize, Hornsby, Musial, Rip Collins, Jack Clark, Dick Allen and Ken Boyer) have hit that many in a season.

■ Big Mac hit 27 more home runs than previous Cardinals record-holder Johnny Mize, in 1940. Only 14 Cardinal players have hit as many as 27 in a season.

■ Only four players on the Cardinals' final-day 1998 roster (Ron Gant, Willie McGee, Brian Jordan and Ray Lankford) had hit as many as 70 home runs in their career.

■ McGwire's 70 home runs traveled a combined distance of 29,598 feet—higher than Mount Everest.

■ McGwire and Sammy Sosa combined for 136 home runs, topping the best two-player single-season total of 115 by Yankees Maris and Mickey Mantle in 1961.

■ McGwire homered every 7.3 at-bats in 1998, Sosa every 9.7. Ruth homered every 9.0 at-bats in 1927 and Maris every 9.7 at-bats in 1961.

■ McGwire's 162 walks equaled the second-highest total in major league history—by Ted Williams in 1947 and '49. Ruth, the record-holder, hit 41 homers when he walked 170 times in 1923. When Ruth put his 60 on the board in '27, he walked 138 times.

■ Despite going to greater lengths than any other hitter, McGwire had 317 occasions in which he didn't put the ball in play: He had 155 strikeouts to go with his 162 walks.

■ McGwire's .752 slugging percentage ranked second in National League history, behind only Hornsby's .756 of 1925. McGwire's total ranked seventh overall.

AND THE WINNER IS...: *Cardinals Hall of Fame broadcaster Jack Buck did the postgame honors (above) when McGwire was presented with the prestigious St. Louis Award.*

who remained long after the final out to honor him in postgame ceremonies. After all was said and done on an 83-79 season that became special because of McGwire's exploits, La Russa grasped unsuccessfully for the words to describe what he had witnessed.

"I've tried, believe me, because he provided moment after moment after moment after moment," La Russa said. "You stutter and you search. What you're thinking, I can't explain.

"I wish somebody was able to say it or write it correctly so that everybody could share it. But I tell you, I've struggled. I've even written stuff down. It never comes out even close to the moment, so I give up.

"The guy is ... it's even stranger than fiction, what this man has done and become."

McGwire vs. Sosa: A statistical

HR	Date	Opposing pitcher, Club	Place	Inn.	On base
1	March 31	Ramon Martinez (righthander), Los Angeles	H	5	3
2	April 2	Frank Lankford (righthander), Los Angeles	H	12	2
3	April 3	Mark Langston (lefthander), San Diego	H	5	1
1	April 4	Marc Valdes (righthander), Montreal	H	3	0
4	April 4	Don Wengert (righthander), San Diego	H	6	2
2	April 11	Anthony Telford (righthander), Montreal	A	7	0
5	April 14	Jeff Suppan (righthander), Arizona	H	3	1
6	April 14	Jeff Suppan (righthander), Arizona	H	5	0
7	April 14	Barry Manuel (righthander), Arizona	H	8	1
3	April 15	Dennis Cook (lefthander), New York Mets	A	8	0
8	April 17	Matt Whiteside (righthander), Philadelphia	H	4	1
9	April 21	Trey Moore (lefthander), Montreal	A	3	1
4	April 23	Dan Miceli (righthander), San Diego	H	9	0
5	April 24	Ismael Valdes (righthander), Los Angeles	A	1	0
10	April 25	Jerry Spradlin (righthander), Philadelphia	A	7	1
6	April 27	Joey Hamilton (righthander), San Diego	A	1	1
11	April 30	Marc Pisciotta (righthander), Chicago Cubs	A	8	1
12	May 1	Rod Beck (righthander), Chicago Cubs	A	9	1
7	May 3	Cliff Politte (righthander), St. Louis	H	1	0
13	May 8	Rick Reed (righthander), New York Mets	A	3	1
14	May 12	Paul Wagner (righthander), Milwaukee	H	5	2
15	May 14	Kevin Millwood (righthander), Atlanta	H	4	0
8	May 16	Scott Sullivan (righthander), Cincinnati	A	3	2
16	May 16	Livan Hernandez (righthander), Florida	H	4	0
17	May 18	Jesus Sanchez (lefthander), Florida	H	4	0
18	May 19	Tyler Green (righthander), Philadelphia	A	3	1
19	May 19	Tyler Green (righthander), Philadelphia	A	5	1
20	May 19	Wayne Gomes (righthander), Philadelphia	A	8	1
9	May 22	Greg Maddux (righthander), Atlanta	A	1	0
21	May 22	Mark Gardner (righthander), San Francisco	H	6	1
22	May 23	Rich Rodriguez (lefthander), San Francisco	H	4	0
23	May 23	John Johnstone (righthander), San Francisco	H	5	2
24	May 24	Robb Nen (righthander), San Francisco	H	12	1
25	May 25	John Thomson (righthander), Colorado	H	1	0
10	May 25	Kevin Millwood (righthander), Atlanta	A	4	0
11	May 25	Mike Cather (righthander), Atlanta	A	8	2
12	May 27	Darrin Winston (lefthander), Philadelphia	H	8	0
13	May 27	Wayne Gomes (righthander), Philadelphia	H	9	1
26	May 29	Dan Miceli (righthander), San Diego	A	9	1
27	May 30	Andy Ashby (righthander), San Diego	A	1	0
14	June 1	Ryan Dempster (righthander), Florida	H	1	1
15	June 1	Oscar Henriquez (righthander), Florida	H	8	2
16	June 3	Livan Hernandez (righthander), Florida	H	5	1
17	June 5	Jim Parque (lefthander), Chicago White Sox	H	5	1
28	June 5	Orel Hershiser (righthander), San Francisco	H	1	1
18	June 6	Carlos Castillo (righthander), Chicago White Sox	H	7	0
19	June 7	James Baldwin (righthander), Chicago White Sox	H	5	2
20	June 8	LaTroy Hawkins (righthander), Minnesota	A	3	0
29	June 8	Jason Bere (righthander), Chicago White Sox	A	4	1
30	June 10	Jim Parque (lefthander), Chicago White Sox	A	3	2
31	June 12	Andy Benes (righthander), Arizona	A	3	3
21	June 13	Mark Portugal (righthander), Philadelphia	A	6	1
22	June 15	Cal Eldred (righthander), Milwaukee	H	1	0
23	June 15	Cal Eldred (righthander), Milwaukee	H	3	0
24	June 15	Cal Eldred (righthander), Milwaukee	H	7	0
25	June 17	Bronswell Patrick (righthander), Milwaukee	H	4	0
32	June 17	Jose Lima (righthander), Houston	A	3	0
33	June 18	Shane Reynolds (righthander), Houston	A	5	0
26	June 19	Carlton Loewer (righthander), Philadelphia	H	1	0
27	June 19	Carlton Loewer (righthander), Philadelphia	H	5	1
28	June 20	Matt Beech (lefthander), Philadelphia	H	3	1
29	June 20	Toby Borland (righthander), Philadelphia	H	6	2
30	June 21	Tyler Green (righthander), Philadelphia	H	4	0
31	June 24	Seth Greisinger (righthander), Detroit	A	1	0
34	June 24	Jaret Wright (righthander), Cleveland	A	4	0
35	June 25	Dave Burba (righthander), Cleveland	A	1	0
32	June 25	Brian Moehler (righthander), Detroit	A	7	0
36	June 27	Mike Trombley (righthander), Minnesota	A	7	1

Categories	McGwire	Sosa
vs. RHP	55	54
vs. LHP	15	12
Home	38	35
Away	32	31
Day	21	33
Night	49	33
Sunday	10	10
Monday	5	14
Tuesday	16	2
Wednesday	8	14
Thursday	7	3
Friday	11	13
Saturday	13	10
1st inning	11	12
2nd inning	0	2
3rd inning	8	8
4th inning	13	5
5th inning	9	12
6th inning	2	8
7th inning	10	6
8th inning	9	9
9th inning	4	4
10th inning	1	0
11th inning	1	0
12th inning	2	0
Solo	33	37
Two-run	28	19
Three-run	7	7
Grand slams	2	3
2-HR games	8	10
3-HR games	2	1
No outs	23	16
One out	21	20
Two outs	26	30
With team losing	25	28
Score tied	25	17
Team leading	20	21
Team record	34-24	30-24
Game-tying HRs	6	7
Go-ahead HRs	30	20
March	1	0
April	10	6
May	16	7
June	10	20
July	8	9
August	10	13
September	15	11
vs. D'backs	4	5
vs. Braves	2	3
vs. Cubs	7	0
vs. ChiSox	2	3

profile

Categories	McGwire	Sosa
vs. Reds	1	4
vs. Indians	2	0
vs. Rockies	2	3
vs. Tigers	0	2
vs. Marlins	7	4
vs. Astros	5	4
vs. Royals	1	0
vs. Dodgers	4	1
vs. Brewers	4	12
vs. Twins	1	1
vs. Expos	6	3
vs. Mets	4	2
vs. Phillies	5	8
vs. Pirates	3	2
vs. Cardinals	0	3
vs. Padres	5	3
vs. Giants	5	3
On grass	60	57
On turf	10	9
Pre-All Star	37	33
Post-All Star	33	33
0-0 Count	11	3
1-0 Count	8	12
2-0 Count	5	2
3-0 Count	0	0
0-1 Count	6	10
1-1 Count	9	2
2-1 Count	8	8
3-1 Count	2	4
0-2 Count	4	3
1-2 Count	7	5
2-2 Count	8	8
3-2 Count	2	9
To LF	34	12
To LCF	20	22
To CF	13	10
To RCF	3	12
To RF	0	10
Total distance (feet)	29598	26869
Average (by feet)	422.8	407.1
Longest (by feet)	545	500
350 and below	3	5
351-375	12	15
376-400	8	10
401-425	16	14
426-450	11	14
451-475	10	3
476-500	5	5
501-525	3	0
526 and longer	2	0

HR	Date	Opposing pitcher, Club	Place	Inn.	On base
37	June 30	Glendon Rusch (lefthander), Kansas City	H	7	0
33	June 30	Alan Embree (lefthander), Arizona	H	8	0
34	July 9	Jeff Juden (righthander), Milwaukee	A	2	1
35	July 10	Scott Karl (lefthander), Milwaukee	A	2	0
38	July 11	Billy Wagner (lefthander), Houston	H	11	1
39	July 12	Sean Bergman (righthander), Houston	H	1	0
40	July 12	Scott Elarton (righthander), Houston	H	7	0
41	July 17	Brian Bohanon (lefthander), Los Angeles	H	1	0
36	July 17	Kirt Ojala (lefthander), Florida	A	6	1
42	July 17	Antonio Osuna (righthander), Los Angeles	H	8	0
43	July 20	Brian Boehringer (righthander), San Diego	A	5	1
37	July 22	Miguel Batista (righthander), Montreal	H	8	2
38	July 26	Rick Reed (righthander), New York Mets	H	6	1
44	July 26	John Thomson (righthander), Colorado	A	4	0
39	July 27	Willie Blair (righthander), Arizona	A	6	1
40	July 27	Alan Embree (lefthander), Arizona	A	8	3
41	July 28	Bob Wolcott (righthander), Arizona	A	5	3
45	July 28	Mike Myers (lefthander), Milwaukee	H	8	0
42	July 31	Jamey Wright (righthander), Colorado	H	1	0
43	Aug. 5	Andy Benes (righthander), Arizona	H	3	1
46	Aug. 8	Mark Clark (righthander), Chicago Cubs	H	4	0
44	Aug. 8	Rick Croushore (righthander), St. Louis	A	9	1
45	Aug. 10	Russ Ortiz (righthander), San Francisco	A	5	0
46	Aug. 10	Chris Brock (righthander), San Francisco	A	7	0
47	Aug. 11	Bobby Jones (righthander), New York Mets	H	4	0
47	Aug. 16	Sean Bergman (righthander), Houston	A	4	0
48	Aug. 19	Kent Bottenfield (righthander), St. Louis	H	5	1
48	Aug. 19	Matt Karchner (righthander), Chicago Cubs	A	8	0
49	Aug. 19	Terry Mulholland (lefthander), Chicago Cubs	A	10	0
50	Aug. 20 (1)	Willie Blair (righthander), New York Mets	A	7	0
51	Aug. 20 (2)	Rick Reed (righthander), New York Mets	A	1	0
49	Aug. 21	Orel Hershiser (righthander), San Francisco	H	5	1
52	Aug. 22	Francisco Cordova (righthander), Pittsburgh	A	1	0
50	Aug. 23	Jose Lima (righthander), Houston	H	5	0
53	Aug. 23	Ricardo Rincon (lefthander), Pittsburgh	A	8	0
51	Aug. 23	Jose Lima (righthander), Houston	H	8	0
52	Aug. 26	Brett Tomko (righthander), Cincinnati	A	3	0
54	Aug. 26	Justin Speier (righthander), Florida	H	8	1
53	Aug. 28	John Thomson (righthander), Colorado	A	1	0
54	Aug. 30	Darryl Kile (righthander), Colorado	A	1	1
55	Aug. 30	Dennis Martinez (righthander), Atlanta	H	7	2
55	Aug. 31	Brett Tomko (righthander), Cincinnati	H	3	1
56	Sept. 1	Livan Hernandez (righthander), Florida	A	7	0
57	Sept. 1	Donn Pall (righthander), Florida	A	9	0
56	Sept. 2	Jason Bere (righthander), Cincinnati	H	6	0
58	Sept. 2	Brian Edmondson (righthander), Florida	A	7	1
59	Sept. 2	Rob Stanifer (righthander), Florida	A	8	1
57	Sept. 4	Jason Schmidt (righthander), Pittsburgh	A	1	0
60	Sept. 5	Dennis Reyes (lefthander), Cincinnati	H	1	1
58	Sept. 5	Sean Lawrence (lefthander), Pittsburgh	A	6	0
61	Sept. 7	Mike Morgan (righthander), Chicago Cubs	H	1	0
62	Sept. 8	Steve Trachsel (righthander), Chicago Cubs	H	4	0
59	Sept. 11	Bill Pulsipher (lefthander), Milwaukee	H	5	0
60	Sept. 12	Valerio De Los Santos (lefthander), Milwaukee	H	7	2
61	Sept. 13	Bronswell Patrick (righthander), Milwaukee	H	5	1
62	Sept. 13	Eric Plunk (righthander), Milwaukee	H	9	0
63	Sept. 15 (1)	Jason Christiansen (lefthander), Pittsburgh	H	9	0
63	Sept. 16	Brian Boehringer (righthander), San Diego	A	8	3
64	Sept. 18	Rafael Roque (lefthander), Milwaukee	A	4	1
65	Sept. 20	Scott Karl (lefthander), Milwaukee	A	1	1
64	Sept. 23	Rafael Roque (lefthander), Milwaukee	A	5	0
65	Sept. 23	Rod Henderson (righthander), Milwaukee	A	6	0
66	Sept. 25	Jose Lima (righthander), Houston	A	4	0
66	Sept. 25	Shayne Bennett (righthander), Montreal	H	5	1
67	Sept. 26	Dustin Hermanson (righthander), Montreal	H	4	0
68	Sept. 26	Kirk Bullinger (righthander), Montreal	H	7	1
69	Sept. 27	Mike Thurman (righthander), Montreal	H	3	0
70	Sept. 27	Carl Pavano (righthander), Montreal	H	7	2

St. Louis played 163 games in 1998 (one tie on August 24), with McGwire participating in 155 games.

Chicago played 163 games in 1998 (one game playoff on September 28), with Sosa participating in 159 games.

Riding the wave

In case a ground ball comes bouncing through the house, I have my old baseball glove within reach. My wife one day asked, "Why do you keep that old glove on your desk? And don't give me that stuff about ground balls rebounding through the house."

The Wilson A2000 is a masterpiece of man's creative urge. It sits atop a computer tower—enthroned, beautiful, shimmering with memories. The leather is golden under a patina of black dirt carried away from infields all over central Illinois.

Slide your hand into the A2000. It's 36 years old and a little dry. Yet the leather is soft to the touch. Soft enough to bring back a kid's dreams. The kid imagines the A2000 carrying him toward a ground ball behind second base. To touch the glove after all this time is to. ...

"Honey, I've figured it out, about my ball glove."

"And?"

"It reminds me of when I had hair."

Yes, and hooray! Baseball lets us be kids forever. The novelist W.P. Kinsella wrote: "Within the baselines, anything can happen. Tides can reverse, oceans can open. That's why they say, 'The game is never over until the last man is out.' Colors can change, lives can alter, anything is possible in this gentle, flawless, loving game." Of all that, Mark McGwire is proof.

Throughout the 1998 season, with grace, warmth, passion and inimitable skill, he showed us how much fun the game can be. He put a smile on America's face.

He did it by hitting baseballs higher and farther than anyone else ever had. He became the very incarnation of that great American mythological hero, the home run hitter.

Best of all, the hero made us smile in the most human way of all. He shared his emotions. "What I've accomplished," he said, "is fabulous." True, and said with a tone of wonder, as if someone else had done it.

He touched us with sentiment and generosity. After hopping onto home plate the night of his 62nd home run, the big man lifted high and kissed his young son, Matt, who was in uniform as the Cardinals' batboy. Time and again, McGwire figuratively embraced Roger Maris even as he literally embraced Sammy Sosa. "Riding the wave," McGwire said of his moment, "along with America."

Astonishing, McGwire's work. More astonishing, his effect on the game. Who'd have thought baseball ever again would be happy front-page news?

The 1998 season began less than four years after major league owners, unable to settle a players' strike, canceled a World Series. Neither Hitler nor an earthquake had ever caused so foul a deed. The owners also made plans to play the 1995 season with strikebreakers/incompetents recruited from God only knows where. Such arrogance. Go back to the Black Sox scandal of 1921. Only then was baseball's connection to its fans more tenuous.

Long embittered by two decades of player-owner wars, fans decided that a pox should fall on both their houses. Attendance, interest and prestige were driven down by anger born of betrayal and abandonment.

A lesser game might have foundered. Baseball, as always, simply outlasted the fools who run it. McGwire himself had foreshadowed the game's comeback. He did it late in the 1997 season.

Though he would be a free agent at season's end and had spent less than two months in St. Louis, he signed a three-year contract extension with the Cardinals. His signing came as a surprise at many levels.

Saying he liked playing for St. Louis fans, he did not conduct a bidding war. His contract averages $9.5 million per year, perhaps about $5 million under the value of a player who had hit 110 home runs for the two previous seasons. McGwire also announced he would donate $1 million per year to fund a foundation for abused children. At a press conference, when he came to the part about children, the strongest man in baseball wept.

Whoa. An athlete who honors his city's fans? Who leaves $5 million on the table? Who gives $1 million to kids whose lives bring him to tears? Who does all this and can hit home runs out of any park, including Yellowstone?

Small wonder, then, that as McGwire chased Babe Ruth's 60 and Roger Maris' 61, baseball fans opened wide their arms to him. And all of baseball profited from the example. Suddenly, those scoundrels of '94 became heroes in '98.

Even in Chicago, it happened for the delightful Sosa. Cubs fans used to call him a whiner who struck out too often and produced too little to earn the adulation and money he demanded. But by the end of the '98 season, when he had chased McGwire across the landscape, he took Wrigley Field curtain calls to chants of "Sam-mee! Sam-mee!" He owned those parts of Chicago not taken by Michael Jordan.

Such a summer, 1998, the sweetest ever in baseball, so sweet that for a neat little while, baseball heroes bumped a presidential scoundrel to the bottom of our front pages.

This is life as life should be.

Thank you, Mr. McGwire.

Dave Kindred is a contributing editor for THE SPORTING NEWS.